Scorpion

Animal
Series editor: Jonathan Burt

Already published

Albatross Graham Barwell · *Ant* Charlotte Sleigh · *Ape* John Sorenson · *Badger* Daniel Heath Justice
Bear Robert E. Bieder · *Bee* Claire Preston · *Beetle* Adam Dodd · *Beaver* Rachel Poliquin
Bison Desmond Morris · *Camel* Robert Irwin · *Cat* Katharine M. Rogers · *Chicken* Annie Potts
Cockroach Marion Copeland · *Cow* Hannah Velten · *Crocodile* Dan Wylie · *Crow* Boria Sax
Deer John Fletcher · *Dog* Susan McHugh · *Dolphin* Alan Rauch · *Donkey* Jill Bough
Duck Victoria de Rijke · *Eagle* Janine Rogers · *Eel* Richard Schweid · *Elephant* Dan Wylie
Falcon Helen Macdonald · *Flamingo* Caitlin R. Kight · *Fly* Steven Connor · *Fox* Martin Wallen
Frog Charlotte Sleigh · *Giraffe* Edgar Williams · *Goat* Joy Hinson · *Gorilla* Ted Gott and Kathryn Weir
Guinea Pig Dorothy Yamamoto · *Hare* Simon Carnell · *Hedgehog* Hugh Warwick · *Horse* Elaine Walker
Hyena Mikita Brottman · *Kangaroo* John Simons · *Leech* Robert G. W. Kirk and Neil Pemberton
Leopard Desmond Morris · *Lion* Deirdre Jackson · *Lobster* Richard J. King · *Monkey* Desmond Morris
Moose Kevin Jackson · *Mosquito* Richard Jones · *Moth* Matthew Gandy · *Mouse* Georgie Carroll
Octopus Richard Schweid · *Ostrich* Edgar Williams · *Otter* Daniel Allen · *Owl* Desmond Morris
Oyster Rebecca Stott · *Parrot* Paul Carter · *Peacock* Christine E. Jackson · *Penguin* Stephen Martin
Pig Brett Mizelle · *Pigeon* Barbara Allen · *Rabbit* Victoria Dickenson · *Rat* Jonathan Burt
Rhinoceros Kelly Enright · *Salmon* Peter Coates · *Scorpion* Louise M. Pryke · *Seal* Victoria Dickenson
Shark Dean Crawford · *Sheep* Philip Armstrong · *Skunk* Alyce Miller · *Snail* Peter Williams
Snake Drake Stutesman · *Sparrow* Kim Todd · *Spider* Katarzyna and Sergiusz Michalski
Swallow Angela Turner · *Swan* Peter Young · *Tiger* Susie Green · *Tortoise* Peter Young
Trout James Owen · *Vulture* Thom van Dooren · *Walrus* John Miller and Louise Miller
Whale Joe Roman · *Wolf* Garry Marvin

Scorpion

Louise M. Pryke

REAKTION BOOKS

To my nephew, Darcy Gordon Jones, the Little Scorpio

Published by
REAKTION BOOKS LTD
Unit 32, Waterside
44–48 Wharf Road
London N1 7UX, UK
www.reaktionbooks.co.uk

First published 2016
Copyright © Louise M. Pryke 2016

Printed and bound in China by 1010 Printing International Ltd

A catalogue record for this book is available from the British Library

ISBN 9 781 78023 592 9

Contents

Introduction:
Shining a Light on Scorpions

Since ancient times, scorpions have captured the imagination of humans. While scorpions and humans have coexisted for thousands of years, the image of the scorpion retains a sense of mystery and danger. In art, media and myth, the small yet distinctively statured scorpion is often depicted as having a ferocious and uncompromising nature. The Carthaginian author Tertullian (*c.* 160–225 CE) provided this description:

> So this is the scorpion, its row of knots forming a delicate, poisonous vein imbued with venom on the inside, rising up in a curved assault, it draws its barbed spear to its full height, in the manner of a war machine.[1]

Tertullian gives this account while explaining how the Roman catapult, Scorpion, received its name. The Scorpion was a piece of Roman artillery that could be operated by one person, yielding a powerfully destructive result over a range as great as 400 m (1,300 ft). The Scorpion catapult's imposing size–to–impact ratio gives an insight into the perception of its namesake animal. Yet, despite the scorpion's hostile reputation, most are not aggressive. They are generally nocturnal by nature, so the scorpion hides in burrows and crevices during the day, staying away from the light.

Black scorpion.

Scorpions are exceptional and diverse creatures. One of their most impressive aspects is the ability to adapt to changing habitats. Recent studies have discovered that some species of scorpion can survive even under extreme environmental conditions. Their toughness is legendary – scorpions have been shown to be able to survive freezing temperatures and submersion in water for up to two days. In drier habitats, some have been known to last for twelve months without food. Further, they are known to be one of the few creatures able to withstand ionizing radiation at nuclear test sites. In many ways, these small arthropods can be considered to be 'super-adapters', surviving for hundreds of millions of years with very few changes to their form, and populating every continent – with the exception of Antarctica.

The relationship between humans and scorpions has been a complicated one since the earliest records, perhaps unsurprisingly given the wide territorial spread of both species. While less than 1 per cent of known scorpion species have venom capable of killing humans, the hazardous aspect of the scorpion dominates its image. Scorpions inspire fear and fascination in inverse proportion to their diminutive size. This is not without reason – even in modern times, scorpion stings are a genuine public health issue in many underdeveloped tropical and subtropical countries. More than 1.2 million people per year are estimated to be stung by scorpions, resulting in over 3,000 deaths.[2] In recent times, the perilous relationship between humans and scorpions has intensified for the scorpion, with several species in danger of extinction.

The focus of this book is the relationship between humans and scorpions, from ancient times to the modern world. While scorpions are often depicted fearsomely, there is a great diversity of human reactions to scorpions in various cultures and at different

Scorpio orientalis, from *Insecten-Belustigung,* by August Johann von Rosenhof (1705–1759).

8

Tab. LXV.

Fig. 2.

Fig. 1.

times in history. Scorpions have held revered roles in religious cult and ritual, and are frequently depicted as playing a protective role for people, gods or the natural environment. It seems fitting that this survivor from prehistoric times is featured in some of our most ancient works of myth and literature. Images of scorpions appear in some of the world's oldest written records, including cave paintings. A hybrid creature, part human and part scorpion, plays a guardian's role in the world's oldest literary epic, the Mesopotamian *Epic of Gilgamesh*. Scorpion imagery appears in artistic works as diverse as Shakespeare's tragedy *Macbeth* and the video game franchise *Mortal Kombat*. From ancient Egypt to modern films, the scorpion can be seen to have lasting links to kingship in human thought. The scorpion's habit of carrying its young on its back is likely to be the cause of the animal's perceived link to motherhood – although the mother scorpion's occasional behaviour of eating its young makes this connection a little surprising!

The high number of fatalities from scorpionism (scorpion envenomation), along with the creature's natural elusiveness and

The desert scorpion, *Androctonus australis*.

A red bark scorpion.

nocturnal habits, have made the scorpion a popular villain in film and narrative. From giant prehistoric monsters in the horror classic *The Black Scorpion* (1957) to an exotic means of torture in the James Bond film *Die Another Day* (2002), the lethality and menace of the scorpion dominate its public image. Whether portrayed as ancient guardians, symbols of royalty or as the sidekick of a supervillain, one feature unites human perceptions of the scorpion – an awareness of its natural power. The diversity of human responses to scorpions through history and in media, from fear to reverence, provides a lens through which to express our anxieties about the uncompromising and often dangerous power of nature.

Perceptions of scorpions throughout history usually begin with an acknowledgement of the scorpion's natural power, then evolve into positive (guarding) or negative (dangerous) interpretations of that force. However, there is a significant variation to the pattern, which is focused on the appreciation of the scorpion's intractable nature and its natural completeness. This appreciation is best expressed through the famous story of the Scorpion and the Frog.

Asian forest scorpion in Khao Yai National Park, Thailand.

The folktale of the Scorpion and the Frog is of uncertain authorship and exists in a number of forms, but it is often told in this way: Scorpion wishes to cross a river, but is unable to swim. The scorpion goes to the frog, who he knows to be a capable swimmer, and asks for a ride across the water. Frog says, 'No! If I give you a ride on my back, you'll sting me.' Scorpion responds, 'It would not be in my interest to sting you! As I'll be on your

Compsobuthus acutecarinatus, scorpion from the Buthidae family, which is found only in Yemen and Oman.

Akan weight from Ghana in the shape of a scorpion.

back, we would both then drown.' Frog thinks this over for a while, but he then accepts Scorpion's deal. Scorpion climbs onto Frog's back, and together they enter the water. When Frog is halfway across the river, he feels a stinging pain in his side and realizes that the scorpion has stung him after all, despite their earlier conversation and agreement. As both Frog and Scorpion sink beneath the waves, Frog cries out, 'Why did you sting me, Scorpion? For now, we both will drown!' Scorpion replies, 'I can't help it, it's in my nature.'

In the story of the Scorpion and the Frog, the scorpion symbolizes the enduring power of a creature's own nature – even to the point of self-destruction. The fabled scorpion's destructive nature ironically overrides its own biological imperative to live. For humans, even as we live in an increasingly technological and civilized world, our animality continues to inform our actions – as it does for the scorpion. The dangerous power of nature, often expressed through depictions of menacing scorpions, is not always found beyond humankind.

1 A Basic Guide to the Biology of Scorpions

We say that the dove invented the kiss, but it has a precursor: the scorpion.
Jean-Henri Fabre

Scorpions are among the earth's most remarkable creatures. When examining the biological distinctiveness of the scorpion, it is simply impossible not to be impressed by the extremities conquered by this pocket-sized arthropod. Gary Polis, the legendary entomologist and scorpion specialist, best expressed this quality of the scorpion, saying:

> When you talk about scorpions, you tend to use a lot of words like 'the only known example,' 'the first,' 'the largest.' It's just one gee-whiz fact after another.[1]

For this reason, it is easy for the non-specialist to develop an appreciation and enthusiasm for the unique biology of scorpions. This chapter considers the life cycle of the scorpion, its predators and prey, and its unique physical features. The famous 'mating dance' of the scorpion is surveyed, as well as the impact of the female's cannibalism of the male in some species. We will also consider the history of the exciting field of scorpiology.

Illustration from
*The Standard
Natural History,*
ed. John Sterling
Kingsley (1884).

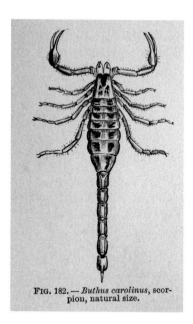

FIG. 182. — *Buthus carolinus,* scorpion, natural size.

Juvenile black
Indian scorpion.

Scorpions are very diverse animals, with more than 1,800 known species. It is estimated that there may be around 7,000 species of scorpion, with new species being discovered every year.[2] Buthidae is the most widely distributed scorpion family, as well as being the largest with more than 531 species.[3] Although scorpions are most commonly associated with arid environments, nearly half of the described species occur in the Neotropical region (also known as the South American region), an area known for its tropical rainforests. Finding new species of scorpion is a difficult and frequently dangerous activity, and ultraviolet light is the method often employed to find the fluorescent, nocturnal scorpion. It is used to good effect in deserts, though it is not as equally effective in tropical forests. This means that the number of species dwelling in rainforest environments is likely to be greater than present estimates suggest.[4] In 2002 two new species of scorpion were discovered using the method of insecticidal fogging from the forest canopy in the region of Manaus in Brazil, and these are likely to be the first species of scorpion discovered to live exclusively in this area.[5] Scientific knowledge of the types of scorpions living in canopies remains an area of study where next to nothing is known.

The rainforests of South America are home to the highest diversity of plants and animals in the world, and scorpions have already proved to have an important role to play in conservation efforts in this region. South American tropical scorpions have been found to exhibit a high degree of endemism (which means that a species is unique to a defined region), and their distinctive behaviours and biologies make them especially important animals for defining priority areas for conservation.[6] The scientific study of the biodiversity of scorpions has already contributed to

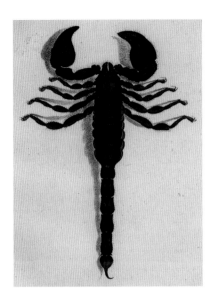

J.F.W. Herbst, plate 1 from *Natursystem der Ungeflügelten Insekten*, c. 1800.

the formation of conservation recommendations in a core area of the tropical Andes – a region believed to be the epicentre for the global diversity of scorpions.[7]

The many species of scorpion contain an extremely diverse arsenal of venom. Scorpion venoms have only in recent years begun to be recognized as a rich source of new medicinal products in the Western world. The toxic compounds present in scorpion venom show great variability, which is perhaps due to the importance of effective venom in the scorpion's adaptations to new environments, adaptations which have taken place over hundreds of millions of years. Scorpion venoms embody a complex mixture of peptides and proteins; the venom of one scorpion species may contain more than 100 different peptides. It is estimated that venoms from all animals may contain more than twenty million different peptides, and of these millions over

Euscorpius in southern France.

Hottentotta jayakari scorpion in the wild.

150,000 are believed to be produced in the venom glands of the currently known scorpion species. Approximately 900 scorpion venom peptides have been identified to date, a figure comprising less than 1 per cent of the estimated total. Continuing research on scorpion venom is important for extending our understanding of the earth's biodiversity; for insights into how venom affects prey; and for the potential development of new antivenoms and medicines.[8]

CLASSIFICATION

To study an animal will always require consideration of how to distinguish that animal from others – how it is like and unlike other creatures. George Henry Lewes, the English philosopher, famously said that science is the systematic classification of experience. While we may apply categories to the scorpion, the science of scorpiology is still in its early stages. Although there are now reasonably sound parameters for the classifications of scorpions, these parameters will likely change to better fit the natural experience of the scorpion as the field continues to develop.

Scorpions are arthropods, along with spiders, centipedes, insects and any other invertebrate animal with an exoskeleton. As arthropods, scorpions exist in a category of organisms which are the most successful and diversified group of creatures on the planet; the majority of organisms known to science are arthropods.[9] They are members of the subphylum Chelicerata, having chelicerae, which are distinctive mouthparts lined with teeth along the inner edges and positioned in front of their mouths. These are used for grabbing and crushing their prey's harder body parts. The scorpion's body is divided into two sections, a cephalothorax (also known as a prosoma) and an abdomen, or opisthosoma. The cephalothorax makes a dorsal shield, and the abdomen is divided into a pre-abdomen and post-abdomen. The post-abdomen is the tail of the scorpion, and the location of the scorpion's sting, which is also known as its aculeus. The stinger is at the end of the tail, and consists of a swollen ampulla, which contains two glands, and a needle-like stinger with separate gland openings near the tip.[10] Each scorpion also has a pair of chelate pedipalps, or pincers, which are the largest parts and which extend from the front of its body. The scorpion's tail and its pincers give the creature its distinctive, easily identifiable silhouette.

Like spiders, scorpions are classed as arachnids, with both groups of animals having four pairs of true legs. Scorpions represent an unusually small group of arachnids with a limited number of genera and species: around 184 genera and approximately

The yellow scorpion, *Buthus occitanus*, perched on a branch.

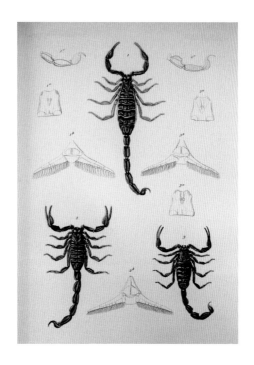

Anatomy of three brown scorpions, from *Animaux nouveaux ou rares* (1855), Francis de Castelnau's record of his expedition to South America.

Some colourful arachnids, from F. É. Guérin-méneville, *Dictionnaire pittoresque d'histoire naturelle et des phénomènes de la nature* (1833–40).

1,900 known species.[11] This is a very small number, especially compared to the scorpions' 'sister' group, spiders, which has over 31,000 species. It seems remarkable that scorpions can be grouped into such relatively small numbers of species and genera, especially when one considers that they are some of the world's most ancient animals, and are known to cover such a wide expanse of territory on earth.

Scorpions have an extremely wide geographical distribution, being present on all the continents except Antarctica.[12] Within this expansive geographical range, scorpions are not randomly dispersed. Instead, particular species are generally found in specific habitats.[13] These habitats show impressive variety; some

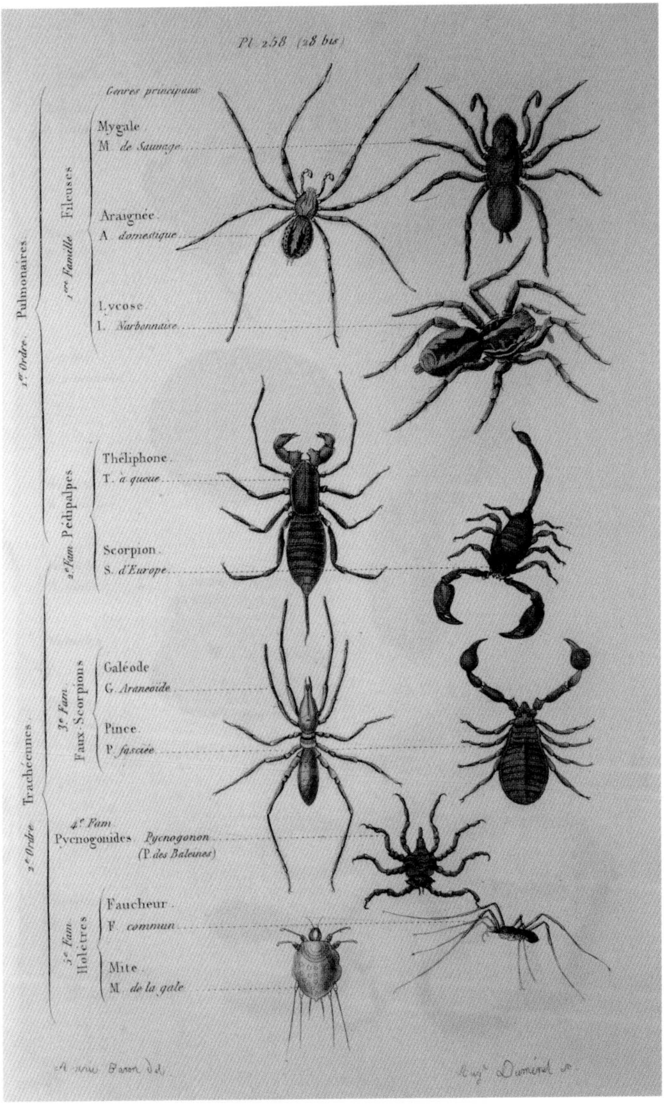

Pl. 258 (28 bis)

Genres principaux

1er Ordre. Pulmonaires.

1re Famille. Fileuses

Mygale
M. de Sauvage.

Araignée
A. domestique

Lycose
L. Narbonnaise

2e Fam. Pédipalpes

Théliphone.
T. à queue

Scorpion.
S. d'Europe

2e Ordre. Trachéennes

3e Fam. Faux-Scorpions

Galéode
G. Araneoide

Pince
P. fasciée

4e Fam.
Pycnogonides Pycnogonon
(P. des Baleines)

5e Fam. Holètres

Faucheur.
F. commun

Mite
M. de la gale

A. van Baron del.   Eug. Dumenil sc.

scorpions can be found in deserts, while others are found along ocean shorelines, mountain ranges, in caves and even in trees.[14] In 2011 the tree-dwelling scorpion *Urophonius tumbensis* was discovered living in the trees of the temperate forests of southern Chile.[15] This South American scorpion has been observed climbing as high as 6 m (20 ft) from the ground, while an Australian scorpion native to pine forests has been found more than 35 m (115 ft) above ground.[16] The ability of scorpions to disperse in a more consistent manner throughout their geographical environment is thought to be limited by three main features – their inability to swim, their dependence on particular types of habitats and their poor phoretic ability (an organism's capacity to form symbiotic relationships in which one organism transports another organism of a different species).

The highest numbers of scorpion genera are found in desert environments, followed by mountainous areas and then tropical habitats. Their preferred microhabitats include burrows, which

Scorpion, *Euscorpius carpathicus*, in a litter of leaves.

The desert scorpion, *Androctonus australis.*

can exceed a depth of 1 m (3.3 ft), spaces under logs and stones, and in rock crevices.[17] When in a fitting habitat, scorpions can be plentiful; densities of one scorpion per square metre were reported for the Middle Eastern *Leiurus quinquestriatus*, known as the death stalker, and of eight to twelve per square metre for *Serradigitus littoralis* from Baja California, Mexico.[18] Scorpions are indeed efficient creatures, capable of successfully adapting to diverse conditions and environments.

LIFE CYCLE

Scorpions are among the most long-lived of arthropods. Some can live for up to 30 years, which is longer than any spider (including the somewhat alarmingly enduring tarantula) or insect, and

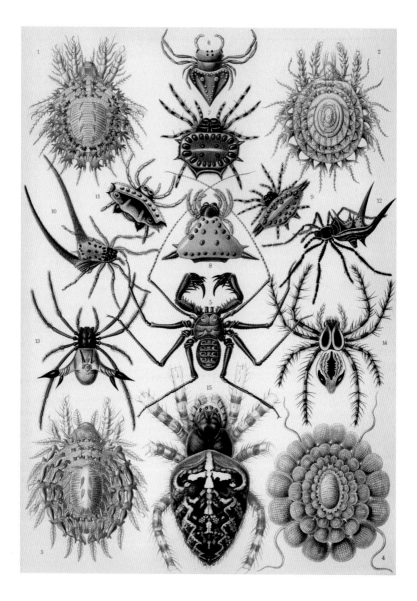

longer than many birds and mammals as well. The relatively long lifespans of scorpions make it difficult to effectively study their life cycles. Lorenzo Prendini, Curator of the Division of Invertebrate Zoology at the American Museum of Natural History, in New York, explained the problem in this way:

Ernst Haeckel, plate 66, 'Arachnida', from *Kunstformen der Natur* (Art Forms in Nature, 1904).

> [Scorpions] are very long-lived, unlike a lot of insects. If you want to do life history studies and things like that, you want things that grow and turn over quite rapidly. Well these guys [many of them] live for years and years, so they don't lend themselves to student projects.[19]

Additional barriers to better understanding the life cycles of scorpions include the animals' nocturnal activity patterns, the general difficulty of finding them in inhospitable and often subterranean environments, and the troubles involved in keeping and observing the creatures in captivity.

Among the arthropods, scorpions have a life cycle that is the most similar to that of humans. Their lives have a surprising number of parallels with our own – they have a relatively long life span, bear live young, have long periods of gestation and a period of maternal care. The scorpion's ability to bear live young is unusual among the arachnids, which typically lay eggs, and which in spiders later hatch into spiderlings (a baby scorpion is called a scorpling). These nascent arthropods usually arrive in litters of around ten to twenty in number, but litters containing more than 100 scorplings occur in some species.

THE SURPRISING SEX LIVES OF SCORPIONS

'Kissing', dancing, handstands, sexual stinging and cannibalism – scorpion mating is a delicate and dangerous affair. Scorpions generally breed through sexual reproduction, and the unique process of 'scorpion sex' involves several remarkable features. One of the most famous aspects of scorpion courtship is a complicated mating ritual known as the *promenade-à-deux* (walking pair). This can be considered a type of mating dance, which is 'led' by the male scorpion.

Despite the attractive French name, the *promenade-à-deux* is quite a violent means of procreation. It is commenced when a male and female scorpion meet. Usually, the process is initiated by the male scorpion, although the female scorpion draws males of the species to her by releasing attractive pheromones. The close proximity of a female leads the male to exhibit a behaviour called 'juddering', which is a kind of vibration involving the scorpion's whole body. He may also tap his pedipalps on the ground. The pre-*promenade* juddering of the male has been shown to be sensed by the females of some species, who then begin courtship behaviour in a series of 'mating attacks', which involve fast and physical encounters between the mating pair.[20]

Next, the male scorpion grabs on to the female, using his pedipalps to grip hold of hers. Sometimes this part of the process takes a few tries, as the male scorpion may miss his target and inadvertently grasp a leg or other body part. Once the scorpions have clasped hold of each other's pincers, the *promenade-à-deux* begins. The male's juddering may continue throughout the *promenade*, which can be as brief as several minutes or continue for over two days. Typically the courtship and mating process itself takes between half an hour to an hour, and in this time the mating pair may travel over 25 m (82 ft).[21] Juddering is highly ritualized behaviour which may help with species recognition, or possibly motivate the female so she is willing to participate in mating. Alternatively, it may be a side effect of the male's sexual excitement.[22] The male scorpion 'leads' the dance, pushing and

pulling the female around by using his grip on her pedipalps. It is thought that this dance-like behaviour is a means of the male scorpion finding the most suitable terrain for him to deploy his genetic material in his spermatophore, a package filled with spermatozoa, which is transferred to the female during the mating process.

During the mating 'dance', some species of scorpions may 'kiss' by joining the chelicerae in front of their mouths. While appearing to kiss, the male scorpion performs a cheliceral massage, by holding and kneading the female's chelicerae with his own. It is thought that this massaging behaviour from the male helps to calm the female and make her more docile at a crucial stage in the mating ritual.[23] Suppressing the aggression of the female during the sexual encounter is perhaps to the advantage of the male scorpion – it may make her less likely to eat him afterwards. The scorpion's sexual sting is another famous behaviour that is thought to be utilized by the male to increase his chances of surviving the sexual encounter. This is also known as the 'aphrodisiac sting'.[24] The male punctures the female's body with his sting, leaving the sting imbedded inside her for up to twenty minutes. It is very difficult to be certain whether the sexual sting includes the deployment of the male scorpion's venom into his mate. If so, this envenomation may drug the female, once again boosting the male's chance of a successful post-coital escape.

After a suitable location has been determined by the male's *promenade*, he will deposit his spermatophore, touching the ground with his genital appendage. However, he must still use his pedipalps to guide the female to his genetic material, and then drag her through the capsule of sperm, which is picked up in the female's genital opening. The female then does a type of head-stand, which opens the valves of her genitalia and allows her to

Kock scorpion, *Centruroides infamatus*, which is found only in Mexico.

absorb the contents of the spermatophore. Once the sperm is inside the female, the male scorpion leaves the area as quickly as possible or he may be caught by his mate and eaten. The risk of cannibalism is not present in all scorpion species – emperor scorpions have been reported to cohabit and raise their young together in harmony for periods of over two years. It should be noted that scorpion mating rituals are not foolproof, with cases of mistaken identity having been observed. Although only scorpions of the same species can successfully mate, 'mating' pairs of scorpions from different species and genera at times engage in courtship and *promenade* behaviour.

Female scorpions of some species are capable of having multiple litters from a single sexual encounter. In a few species, the scorpions reproduce without the involvement of male partners through parthenogenesis. This is a form of reproduction where offspring are produced without the input of sperm to fertilize the egg. It is a rare behaviour among the arachnid group, but has been observed in species of scorpion such as *Tityus serrulatus* from Brazil, *Tityus columbianus* from Colombia and *Tityus metuendus* from Peru and Brazil, as well as *Liocheles australasiae*. While *Liocheles australasiae* has a wide geographical dispersion through Australia and Asia, only female scorpions of this species have been discovered in Asia, with males seen only rarely in Australia.[25] This may be due to the common occurrence of thelytokous parthenogenesis, which is a type of parthenogenesis where only female litters are produced. The only exception to this gynocentric trend in scorpions that produce offspring without a mate is *Tityus metuendus*, in which arrhenotoky (all-male broods) has been observed.[26]

Once the female is inseminated, she may be pregnant for between two and eighteen months, but stress during the pregnancy may cause her to reabsorb the embryos. Some females may be pregnant for most of their lives. A recent study of striped bark scorpions found that the females were gestating for 80 per cent of the year.[27] The females of this species, common to northern Mexico and southern parts of the United States, were also bigger, slower and more likely to sting than males. In the study's temperament test, 75 per cent of the female bark scorpions attempted to sting metal forceps used to hold them, whereas none of the male scorpions did. The authors of the study explained the female's aggressive reaction by reasoning that stinging is not the ideal response to a predator for a scorpion; the production of venom has a metabolic cost, and the production of new venom takes time, leaving the scorpion vulnerable. If escape without stinging were possible, this would likely be a better option. However, the decreased speed and manoeuvrability of a pregnant scorpion may make stinging seem a good alternative to fleeing.

Scorpions give birth either seasonally or year round. In temperate climates, birthing occurs in the warmer months of spring and summer. In tropical regions, there is no favoured time for birth. Our understanding of the behaviours involved in scorpion birth is still developing; the births often occur in protected places in the natural environment, so most scientific knowledge of the subject is based on experiences with laboratory animals. Just prior to giving birth, the female raises her body off the ground in a 'stilting' posture. The mother's first two pairs of legs may form a 'birth basket', catching the baby scorpions as they drop from her genital opercula. The number of young is hard to estimate, even when watching the scorpion give birth, as this can take over 24 hours. Some of the young may disappear during the parturition process, possibly due to having been eaten.[28] The surviving scorplings then climb up the mother's legs and pincers to settle upon her back, where they will ride until after their first moult. Arthropods must shed their skin to grow, which means they grow in short bursts rather than gradually over time. Scorpions grow in stages called instars. A few days after their first moult (or once reaching their second instar), the scorplings will begin to leave their mother. The early association of mother scorpion and scorpling is crucial to their development, as the scorplings have been shown to absorb water from their mother while on her back.[29] Unlike their fully grown relatives, scorplings do not have a waterproof cuticle that prevents high rates of water loss, so this ability to obtain fluids in the first instar is necessary for the progeny to survive. Their position on their mother's back also helps to shield the young from predators, which may include male scorpions and unfertilized female scorpions. Females of some species have been shown to pick up fallen young and help them to return to their place on her back. However, if the baby scorpions stay with their mother too long after their first moult, she may eat them. Rarely, in some species such as the chactoid scorpion, *Scorpio maurus palmatus*, the scorplings and their mother will reside together for long periods of time.

Giant hairy scorpion, *Hadrurus arizonensis*, the largest scorpion in North America.

In addition to the risk of cannibalism, numerous other creatures prey upon scorpions. More than 100 vertebrate and 30 invertebrate predators have been reported to feed on scorpions, with the type of predator varying with the scorpion's geographic location.[30] Despite their tough exoskeleton, the abundance of scorpions in many locations and their rich nutrient content make them an appealing choice of prey. Among their vertebrate predators are birds, lizards, mammals, snakes, frogs and toads. Representing the invertebrate predators are other arachnids (such as wolf spiders), centipedes and some insects (usually ants). Most scorpions are captured while exposed on the ground, but some predators, such as coyotes, will dig them up. Baboons, too, have been observed searching under rocks for scorpions. Due to the nocturnal nature of scorpions, a large number (though by no means all) of their predators are nocturnal.

Scorpions have several defensive adaptations to improve their chances of evading predators, such as 'cryptic colouring'

Scorpions such as this can use camouflage to adapt to their surroundings.

34

or camouflage, where the scorpion's hue closely matches its environment, making it difficult for predators to find. Of these adaptations, the scorpion's deadliest form of defence against attack is its sting. All scorpions have stingers at the end of their body, on the metasoma, and all are venomous. To get around this defensive weaponry, some animals have a natural immunity to scorpion venom. These predators include types of snake, mongoose and meerkat. Some animals can actually get a positive effect from the scorpion's sting. Recent research has shown that the grasshopper mouse is resistant to scorpion venom and, quite paradoxically, the venom produces an analgesic (pain-killing) effect on the mouse.[31] The grasshopper mouse survives in harsh desert environments of North America and Mexico, meaning it has most likely evolved the ability to withstand scorpion venom in order to increase its prey options in the extreme climate of the

Black-backed kingfisher eating a scorpion in the Hala-Bala Wildlife Sanctuary, Thailand.

desert. The immunity of the grasshopper mouse is created by two proteins found in a subset of its sensory nerve fibres. Research on the pain-killing effects of scorpion venom has raised the possibility of investigating these proteins for use in the future production of new analgesics for use on humans.

If the predator is not immune to the venom of the scorpion, it may get around it by removing the animal's metasoma, where the sting is located. The elf owl, which lives in southwestern states of North America and in Mexico, is the world's lightest owl and has been described as 'the greatest scorpion killer of all'.[32] These owls have been photographed carrying scorpions back to their nests to feed their young after detaching the stinger. The owl researcher J. David Ligon reported finding four scorpions in the stomach of a single elf owl – each one with its tail removed.[33]

A little-known defensive behaviour of some species of scorpion is the ability to play dead. They also evade predators by inhabiting hard-to-reach hiding places and are notoriously difficult to catch

Striped scorpion blends with the rocky landscape.

The elf owl, a fearsome predator of scorpions and other invertebrates.

unawares. Predators cannot rely on the element of surprise; with up to six pairs of eyes around the front corners of their carapace (a covering on their upper cephalothorax) and an additional pair located on a small central tubercle, scorpions can see both forwards and backwards at the same time.[34] In 2015 scorpiologists made the discovery that a genus of South American scorpions can shed their tails, and part of the gut, to assist with their escape from predators.[35]

Humans present a great threat to many species of scorpion. In recent years, harvesting for the exotic pet trade and souvenirs has left some of the best-known types of scorpion on the Convention on International Trade in Endangered Species (CITES) list. This listing of scorpions by CITES means that some types of scorpion are now recognized as requiring international protection from over-exploitation, for their continued survival in the wild. It has been noted that the rapid growth of the human population, and the ensuing demands of our species on the earth's natural resources, is not ideal to support a complex ecosystem.[36] For scorpions, this results in a reduction of biodiversity due to over-harvesting and habitat degradation. Humans may also prey on scorpions in a more direct manner than impinging on their habitat or collecting them for the black market. In North Africa, there is thought to be a tribe of people known as 'the scorpion-eaters'. In response to an infestation of scorpions, the owner of the affected household will summon a scorpion-eater, who is able to entice the scorpions from their hiding places with soft whistling. Once the lured scorpions have been captured by the scorpion-eater, they are taken away to be eaten. The profession of scorpion-eating is thought to be an inherited one, with the ability restricted to certain families within a village.[37]

The scorpion is an efficient predator capable of ingesting large amounts of food in a short space of time, and excreting very little. They have an extremely low metabolic rate, which means they can survive without food for long stretches of time – sometimes for a period of over a year. The ability to survive starvation is likely a response to the harsh environmental conditions often inhabited by scorpions, and there is some variation between species in how successfully the creatures cope without food. Insects, spiders and other small animals are the usual prey for scorpions. The hunting techniques of the scorpion can be different depending on the species. Most are tactile creatures, which locate their prey through touch and by sensing tremors. They have sensitive hairs lining their pedipalps which alert them to slight changes in air current or vibration. Many species have been observed orienting themselves towards flying insect prey up to 10 cm (4 in.) away, by sensing the prey's movement.

When they sense a change in their environment, scorpions may make a noise by a process called 'stridulation'. This is a low-pitched sound which is audible to humans, described by the legendary naturalist David Attenborough as a kind of hissing noise, which is made by the scorpion rubbing its legs together.[38] Scorpions are not known for having sharp eyesight; in fact, some species are blind. The eyes of scorpions are extremely sensitive, however, to very low levels of light, and they are able to navigate their wild habitats by the faint illumination of the stars.

To catch prey, some scorpions may employ ambush or 'sit and wait' tactics, while others actively search out and chase their

Euscorpius italicus eating a beetle.

prey. The pedipalps are used to grasp hold of the prey and may be used for killing, depending on the size of the catch. Relatively small prey are not killed by stinging, and species of scorpions with larger pedipalps are more likely to use them to crush their victims. Scorpions show an ability to orient the body of their prey prior to feeding, with many seemingly preferring to consume the head first.

If stinging is required, scorpions arch their tail over their body to stab their stinger into the prey, sometimes repeatedly. It was noted above that the scorpion's venom is valuable for its survival and therefore is not expended lightly. Perhaps unsurprisingly, then, the muscles of the stinger allow the scorpion to control how much venom is released into the prey with each sting and even whether the sting will be 'wet' or 'dry'. They are also able to use more venom in high-threat conditions. Impressively, scorpions

Giant metal sculpture of a scorpion battling a grasshopper in the Anza-Borrego Desert State Park, Borrego Springs, California.

can choose the strength of venom injected, inserting either clear (potassium-rich) prevenom or milky (protein-rich) venom.[39] Although the method by which the scorpion regulates the dispersal of its venom and prevenom is at the current time poorly understood, it is possible that there is a difference in purpose between the two fluids. Prevenom may be useful defensively, perhaps to induce localized pain in vertebrates such as mice – animals that frequently make a meal of scorpions.[40] The protracted localized pain following a scorpion sting is thought to be a product of the injection of prevenom. However, the prevenom is also capable on its own of immobilizing insects, so it is additionally useful for prey capture.

Some scorpions, commonly those of the *Parabuthus* genus, are able to squirt their venom to distances of over 1 m (3 ft). Scorpion venom squirted into the eyes is very dangerous and requires medical treatment. A member of this genus, *Parabuthus transvaalicus*, which is native to Botswana, Mozambique, South Africa and Zimbabwe, has somewhat surprisingly been recorded in pet collections in the United States and Europe, despite causing a number of fatalities in Africa and having the large venom sacs that are required for venom squirting.

While humans are not a traditional prey for scorpions, scorpion stings kill thousands of people every year. For every one person killed by a venomous snake, ten are killed by venomous scorpions. It is difficult to get exact figures on the number of scorpion-related deaths, as many of the areas worst affected by scorpionism are in developing nations, or in desert or jungle areas without large medical facilities. However, it is thought that over a million people per year are stung by scorpions, resulting in thousands of deaths.[41] Scorpion venom is heterogeneous, meaning that it varies in composition and effect from species to species. The toxicity of the venom is also variable, with

A scorpion's stinger.

some producing mild flu-like symptoms, and others capable of producing death within an hour.[42] *Centruroides sculpturatus*, also known as the bark scorpion, is common in the southwestern United States and northern Mexico, and its sting causes intense pain, convulsions, frothing at the mouth and respiratory paralysis. As late as the 1940s, the bark scorpion was responsible for more deaths in the state of Arizona than all other venomous creatures combined, including rattlesnakes, spiders, gila monsters and bees.[43]

Scorpion venom may contain a number of different toxins, with neurotoxins being the most potent. *Androctonus australis*, a North African desert scorpion, and *Leiurus quinquestriatus*, the death stalker scorpion, have the most lethal venom of all known scorpions. A person of average size would have a less than 50 per cent chance of surviving the sting of the death stalker. This species is also known to be remarkably resistant to its own venom, with eighteen stings from one *Leiurus* being required to kill another.[44] Scorpion combat is a more sophisticated process than just both creatures lashing indiscriminately at one another – strategy and tactics are part of the battle. It has been observed that when two *Leiurus* scorpions do battle, the stronger animal will attempt to turn its opponent upside down and sting it in the middle of its abdomen. Despite the high resistance of *Leiurus* to its own venom, a sting into the ganglion of the ventral nerve cord results in instant death.[45]

Androctonus australis is a remarkable creature in both its lethality and toughness. This scorpion's venom is considered to be equivalent in potency to that of a black mamba (one of the world's most venomous snakes) and the animal is capable of surviving extreme environmental conditions.[46] While other creatures which inhabit the same desert environment as this scorpion burrow beneath the ground to protect themselves in sandstorms, *Androctonus australis* remains on the surface and has the ability to withstand winds with sufficient speed to strip the paint off steel.[47] Scientists from Jilin University in China have been conducting research to see whether this scorpion's impenetrable armour can be reproduced to increase the longevity of aircraft engines and helicopter rotor blades. Despite (or perhaps because of) the ferocity of the creature's venom, it is one of the top three species of scorpions commonly found in the exotic live animal trade, along with *Pandinus imperator*, emperor scorpions, and *Androctonus amoreuxi*.

Human deaths from scorpion envenomation most often occur in the first 24 hours following a sting, and are usually caused by cardiovascular or respiratory failure. Children and the elderly are most at risk of a fatal outcome from the scorpion's sting; a mortality rate of 10 per cent is reported for untreated school-age children.[48] When considering the gender of the patient, women are more at risk of acquiring stings than men, with a recent five-year Saudi Arabian study finding that women were stung nine times more frequently than men. The lower body weight of females also means they are more susceptible than men to severe symptoms of envenomation. Fortunately, improvements in medical treatments and care, and better public education and programmes to control scorpion populations, have resulted in a substantial decrease in deaths from scorpion envenomation, although further research and planning is needed to increase survival rates, particularly in tropical and subtropical areas such as southern Latin America, Sahelian Africa and southern India.[49]

FLUORESCING

One of the many unique features of the scorpion is its ability to fluoresce under ultraviolet light. Fluorescent chemicals in the scorpion's exoskeleton are thought to be the cause of its glow. All adult scorpions glow under ultraviolet light (for example, the type of light put out by a black light), yet the cause and function of this behaviour is largely a mystery.[50] This remarkable phenomenon was first reported as recently as 1954, and has since had a revolutionary effect on the study of scorpion biology and ecology.[51] There have been many theories formed to attempt to explain this distinctive quality of luminescence in scorpions. It has been suggested that glowing may be a vestigial trait from a more ancient, diurnal species, or that the fluorescence may function as a lure for prey. This latter theory seems unlikely, as recent research has proved that aerial insects (wisely!) attempt to avoid fluorescing scorpions.[52] Further theories are that the glowing serves no function, with the glow being a side effect of metabolic processes, or that the lit-up scorpion is better able to find a mate. This last theory seems plausible, as fluorescing pedipalps on jumping spiders have been shown to be an adaptive advantage in mating.[53] A study published in 2012 has shown that the fluorescence of scorpions affects their perception of light, and may help them to locate shelter in areas with a poor light source.[54]

A scorpion glowing under uv light.

It is seemingly no coincidence that scorpions have survived in more or less the same form for hundreds of millions of years; they are particularly tough animals, able to withstand incredible environmental extremes. Scorpions have a high level of radio-resistance, a fact that was discovered by chance in the mid-twentieth century. In 1960 French scientists were conducting atmospheric (above ground) tests on nuclear weapons at the Reggane Oasis in the Sahara Desert. The exercise was code-named 'Gerboise Bleue' (Blue Desert Rat). Gerboise Bleue carried an explosive yield of 70 kilotons, around four times as powerful as the Hiroshima bomb.[55] The scientists discovered that near ground zero, the only animals that had survived the blast were scorpions, along with a particularly hardy species of beetle. In the field and laboratory tests that followed, it was quickly confirmed that scorpions have an extremely high resistance to ionizing radiation.[56] Further studies have attempted to better understand the natural mechanisms that give scorpions this protection from damage caused by radiation. It seems likely that the scorpion's low oxygen consumption and low metabolic rate help it to withstand damage.[57] However, the exact processes involved in their resistance are not entirely clear at the present time.

Harsh environmental factors can be tolerated by many, but not all, species of scorpion. In contrast to other animal species, the scorpion seems particularly well placed to cope with extreme conditions such as excessive heat and cold, starvation, dehydration and fire. The death stalker scorpion, native to desert areas in North Africa, has the ability to survive for 24 hours at a temperature of 47°C, or 166.6°F; another species, the Israeli gold scorpion (*Scorpio maurus*), can survive temperatures up to 50°C

(122°F). This is among the highest levels of tolerance to heat of all desert-dwelling animals, with only the Arabian camel and some types of reptiles and insects also able to cope with such high temperatures.[58] We do not traditionally associate scorpions with snow; however, certain species of scorpion are able to cope with extremely cold, even freezing, temperatures. A zoologist interviewed by *National Geographic* noted that he froze scorpions in the course of his research, and saw them walk away once they were thawed out the following day.[59] Some types of scorpion can better this accomplishment by surviving freezing for several weeks.[60] The mechanisms which allow the scorpions to survive in icy climates are currently poorly understood, although the North American species *Centruroides vittatus* has been found to have antifreeze substances preventing the formation of ice crystals in its intestine.[61]

Lack of water can be tolerated by most types of scorpion. Without water or food, some members of the Buthidae family can survive for over a year. Drinking is altogether unnecessary for some species of desert scorpion, which are able to gain sufficient fluids from the prey they eat, or even by absorbing fluid from humid soil. While scorpions cope impressively well with a scarcity of water, they can also manage well with an overabundance of it, being able to survive underwater for two days.[62]

A species of scorpion, *Lychas alexandrinus*, native to Australia, a land famous for its devastating bushfires in summer, has been shown to have its population levels unaffected by fire, even with an accompanied decrease in available prey.[63] The recorded numbers of *Lychas alexandrinus* in fire-affected areas of the Tanami Desert were indistinguishable from those in areas that did not experience fire, although it is uncertain how this feat was achieved.

The amazing ability of scorpions to survive in inhospitable conditions adds to their reputation as natural 'super-adaptors', which should be viewed as one of evolution's success stories. Scorpions and their many remarkable features are the focus of the exciting and developing field of scorpiology. The work of scientists over hundreds of years has resulted in the improved understanding and appreciation of scorpions that we have today. However, it seems extraordinary to note that, as a field, scorpiology is a relatively recent discipline. Despite the ancient origins of its subject, it was only in the later part of the twentieth century that the vast majority of our knowledge on scorpions came to light.

When considering the study of scorpions, it is possible to observe the dominance of the animal's stinger in human perception. As noted earlier, the scorpion does not tend to lend itself lightly to study. Many areas where scorpion populations are plentiful are remote and inhospitable. There is the added deterrent of their nocturnal habits, and their preference for either burrowing or choosing an arboreal habitat. While these homes provide shelter and protection for the scorpion, they provide an obstacle for the researcher. The characteristic ability of scorpions to fluoresce under ultraviolet light was only discovered, seemingly by chance, in the 1950s. Prior to this, locating a scorpion subject for study in a dark desert night would have been an unlikely prospect. Although there is an inherent danger in studying some of the more venomous scorpion species, other inhabitants of their favoured terrain, such as the rattlesnake, may prove a further hazard for the nocturnal scorpiologist – and they do not give away their location with luminescence! The difficulties associated with studying scorpions in the wild were noted over 100 years ago. In 1905 the French entomologist Jean-Henri Fabre remarked of his

An emperor scorpion, native to tropical Africa. This species is the one most commonly found as a pet.

desire to see the mating rituals of scorpions in their natural environment:

> If I were not afraid to break my legs at night, between the congestion of their rocky hills, I would like to attend their wedding festival in the delights of freedom.[64]

The known study of scorpions through scientific methodology begins with the Greek philosopher Aristotle (384–322 BCE). A graduate of Plato's academy and tutor to Alexander the Great, Aristotle wrote a collection of scientific works that included considerations on a variety of animals. His *History of Animals* contains several passages on the appearance and habits of the scorpion. Although a great deal of Aristotle's views (scientific and otherwise) have been proven to be grossly inaccurate, the bringing together of such a large amount of zoological information represents an important turning point in the history of the biological sciences. Perhaps for this reason, Aristotle's conclusions stood unchallenged for hundreds of years after they were written, and his writing enjoyed an almost canonical popularity in the Middle Ages.

The first aspect of the scorpion noted by Aristotle is, fairly predictably, its sting:

> Certain insects are furnished with prickers or stings. Some insects have the sting inside, as the bee and the wasp, others outside, as the scorpion; and, by the way, this is the only insect furnished with a long tail. And, further, the scorpion is furnished with claws, as is also the creature resembling a scorpion found within the pages of books.

The next area of interest was the scorpion's method of reproduction:

> The land-scorpion also lays a number of egg shaped grubs, and broods over them. When the hatching is completed, the parent animal, as happens with the parent spider, is ejected and put to death by the young ones; for very often the young ones are about eleven in number.[65]

Here we find a mixture of accurate and inaccurate information. For example, it is the scorpling which is at risk of its parents' cannibalism, rather than the other way around. However, the estimate of eleven offspring is accurate for many species of scorpion, such as *Opistophthalmus wahlbergii* (also known as the hissing scorpion), which usually gives birth to between nine and twelve scorplings. This is also the first recorded observation of the scorpion as viviparous (birthing live young rather than laying eggs). Aristotle's final observation on scorpions is on the varying toxicity of their venom, depending on their geographic location. This observation shows an early awareness of the variability of scorpion venom between species. Aristotle's insight in ascribing variations in toxicity to differences in geographic location potentially makes his study a precursor to the modern field of biogeography.[66]

Pliny the Elder, the Roman naturalist, was concerned primarily with the venomous capabilities of scorpions. In his writings on natural science, he included several remedies against scorpion stings. Despite the well-intentioned aim of these remedies, none sounds terribly appealing! Pliny suggests the consumption of ground-up stones from Egypt or Cyprus as beneficial for scorpion envenomation, along with river-crabs (or their ashes) in the milk of an ass, and the flesh of raw or boiled snails, which could also be applied topically to the site of the wound. Pliny's most interesting comment on scorpions was the observation that some have two tails. A second tail is a developmental abnormality in scorpions, and an ancient drawing of a double-tailed scorpion was found in the tomb of the New Kingdom pharaoh Seti I (1290–1279 BCE).[67] This is likely the first record of a scorpion with two metasomas, more than thirteen centuries before Pliny the Elder.[68]

In the late sixteenth century, the Swiss naturalist Conrad Gessner's landmark work *Historiae animalium* provided the insight that scorpion mothers carry their offspring upon their backs. This observation was also noted by the Dutch naturalist Jan Swammerdam. A student of Gessner, Caspar Wolf, published the first comprehensive monograph on scorpions in 1587.[69] Wolf's original monograph, *De Scorpione*, was published in Latin, with a German translation following two years later.

The development of the first prototypical microscope around 1595 allowed a leap forwards in the research of the natural sciences through improved technology. The influence of the English

Pandinus magrettii.
This species is
native to northeast
Africa.

physicist Robert Hooke's *Micrographia* in 1665 gave further
impetus to the advance of understanding biological structures
and the physiology of organisms. Also in the seventeenth century,
Francesco Redi and Holger Jacobaeus made separate ground-
breaking contributions on scorpions' reproductive biology. Redi,
in particular, was one of the first natural scientists to contradict
the views of Aristotle on the origin of insects, views that were still
extremely influential.[70]

The myth that the scorpion commits suicide when faced with an
inescapable and deadly situation was explored, at the expense of a
great many scorpions, in a study by the biologist Alfred G. Bourne
in 1886.[71] The phenomenon of an animal acting in a manner so
contrary to the biological imperative to survive created a great
deal of interest in scientific circles in the late nineteenth century.
Despite a wide variety of tests, Bourne was unable to replicate the
supposed behaviour in his laboratory specimens.

The mating dance of the scorpion was poetically described in
1905 by Jean-Henri Fabre, in his *Souvenirs entomologiques*. Fabre's
education was largely autodidactic, due to his family's poverty.
However, Fabre's observations of *Buthus occitanus* (the Languedoc

yellow scorpion) are still recognized as containing a high degree of accuracy, proving that, even without a traditional education, passion for a subject combined with knowledge can engender the discovery of large amounts of useful and interesting data.[72] Fabre labelled his scorpions 'cowards' due to their shyness. Although modern scientific studies generally aim to avoid such anthropomorphic descriptions, it is interesting to observe that Fabre's analysis represents a shift away from the predominant view of scorpions as aggressive and dangerous creatures.

Of course, any study on scorpions would be incomplete without acknowledging the field-altering contribution of ecologist, arachnologist and scorpion expert Gary A. Polis. In 1990 Polis produced the work that has become known in the field of entomology as the 'scorpion bible', *The Biology of Scorpions*.[73] This collection of essays covers everything from scorpion neurobiology to folklore, and pushed the field of scorpion science into an exciting new era, while at the same time revitalizing scholarly interest in the study of scorpions.[74] In recent years, the ecological and zoological significance of scorpions has become more widely appreciated. Through the continued work of dedicated scorpiologists, entomologists, arachnologists and ecologists, in years to come we will continue to unravel more of the mysteries surrounding these remarkable and ancient creatures.

2 Scorpions in Prehistory and the Ancient World

> Behold, I give unto you power to tread on serpents and
> scorpions, and over all the power of the enemy: and nothing
> shall by any means hurt you.
> Luke 10:19

Scorpions are among earth's most ancient creatures – in the past
it was popular for scholars to describe them as living fossils.
Although they have experienced some changes in their form,
scorpions' efficiency and ability to adapt has seen them survive
and thrive for a length of time almost incomprehensible in its
vastness. Scorpions existed for hundreds of millions of years
before the arrival of humans in the planet's history. The relationship between scorpions and humans has been a powerful
symbol in human thought since the early stages of some of the
world's most ancient civilizations. The relatively recent arrival
and ongoing development of human societies has also had a
significant impact on scorpions. This chapter compares depictions of the scorpion in some of the most dominant cultures of
the ancient world.

SCORPIONS IN PREHISTORY

When we think of the prehistoric age, our first impulse may be
to consider several well-known species of dinosaur, such as the
triceratops and tyrannosaurus of the Cretaceous Period, and
stegosaurus and diplodocus of the Jurassic Period, rather than
the scuttling arachnid which is the focus of this book. Nonetheless, the scorpion pre-dates all of these famous creatures by

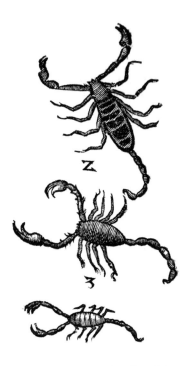

Various scorpions from Ulisse Aldrovandi, *De animalibus insectis* (1638).

hundreds of millions of years. The earliest bipedal member of the Homininae subfamily (of which modern humans are a part) arose around seven million years ago, which means that human-like creatures have existed for less than 1 per cent of the time that scorpions have roamed the earth.

How have scorpions changed over the course of all of this time, and how did they originate? What sort of fossil record do we have to inform us about prehistoric scorpions? We will go back to the beginning, with the evidence available to us, to attempt to answer these questions. The first life on earth began in the ocean long before organisms emerged onto land. During the Silurian Period (beginning around 440 million years ago), the process of terrestrialization – the movement of life from the sea to land – began. This process is clearly one of the most important chapters in the history of our earth. The first types of life to move from water to land were plants. These plants would slowly increase both in size and complexity throughout the succeeding Devonian Period (beginning around 416 million years ago). The initial appearance of plants on land was soon followed by plant- and debris-eating invertebrate animals, such as insects and millipedes. By the end of the Silurian Period, predatory invertebrates such as scorpions and spiders were feeding on the earlier, plant-eating colonists of the land. By the Carboniferous Period (beginning around 358 million years ago), early vertebrates – our four-legged ancestors – had in turn left the water and were feeding on the invertebrates.

The oldest-known scorpions are dated to the Silurian Period. Complete scorpion fossils are, however, very rare and frequently poorly preserved due to the thin leathery nature of their cuticle (external skeleton), creating significant difficulties for their

Representation of Silurian flora.

Fossilized scorpion pincer from the *Gondwanascorpio emzantsiensis*, discovered in South Africa.

study. In addition to the extreme scarcity of fossil scorpions, our understanding of them has, at least until recent times, been limited by the impossibility of gaining information on the creature's internal structures.[1] In 2013 there was a particularly exciting development in the study of prehistoric scorpions, with the discovery of the new species *Gondwanascorpio emzantsiensis* in South Africa. This discovery was made by Dr Robert W. Gess, who revealed that the scorpion is the oldest-known terrestrial animal to have lived in the southern hemisphere. Prior to this discovery, evidence of the earliest colonization of land by animals had come only from the northern hemisphere supercontinent, with no evidence that Gondwana was inhabited by land-living invertebrate animals at such an early stage.[2]

The discovery of *Gondwanascorpio emzantsiensis* marked a significant shift in our understanding of how life developed on earth. *Gondwanascorpio* is thought to have been around 15 cm (6 in.) long and probably looked quite similar to modern scorpions.[3] As a predatory animal, it would have fed on other terrestrial invertebrates (which are currently still being sought by palaeontologists). The discovery of *Gondwanascorpio* implies that plant- and/or detritus-eating invertebrates were also present at this early stage. These invertebrates probably included detritivorous millipedes – creatures that obtain nutrients by consuming dead organic

Fossilized scorpion sting of the 360-million-year-old *Gondwanascorpio emzantsiensis.*

material – primitive plant-eating insects and extinct trigonotarbid arachnids (an extremely ancient extinct group of arachnids). *Gondwanascorpio* would potentially have provided food for early tetrapods (ancestors of reptiles and mammals), which looked like giant salamanders. Although these are thought to have all still been aquatic during the Late Devonian Period, they would have had the ability to grab invertebrates from the undergrowth near the water's edge. Somewhere around this time or during the earliest Carboniferous Period, some tetrapods became predominantly terrestrial. They were predatory, about 1 m (3 ft) long, and would have eaten terrestrial invertebrates, such as early scorpions. In fact, the presence of terrestrial invertebrates would have been an important prerequisite for terrestrialization by vertebrates.[4]

Scorpion terrestrialization has long been an area of scholarly controversy. An aquatic mode of life for prehistoric scorpions was first suggested in 1885 by the self-taught naturalist Robert Parr Whitfield, sparking intense scientific debate.[5] Scorpions were once thought to have developed from an ancient group of arthropods called Eurypterida that varied in size from a few centimetres to more than 2 m (6.6 ft) long.[6] In 2007 the fossilized remains of one of these marine creatures, *Jaekelopterus rhenaniae*, was discovered in Germany. When alive, it is believed the creature may have weighed up to 180 kg (400 lb). Though it was once widely accepted in scientific circles that the earliest scorpions were aquatic, this theory stemmed merely from their remains being found in shallow marine sediments and from their resemblance to eurypterids. Recent findings in the fossil record, along with the reinterpretation of specimens, suggest that this traditional view was not accurate and that the earliest scorpions were terrestrial. First, their presence in marine sediments is always accompanied by the remains of terrestrial plants, suggesting that they were washed in along with land plants. Second, scorpions are closely

The fossilized remains of a now-extinct sea scorpion, *Eurypterus remipes,* from the Silurian Period.

related to spiders, sharing a number of features with them. Some of these features are adaptations to terrestrial life, such as book lungs, bristles (trichobothria) and the structure of their mouthparts. As these characteristics are shared by spiders and scorpions, it is assumed that they were inherited from a common terrestrial ancestor, one that pre-dates both spiders and scorpions.

Palaeoscorpius devonicus, long thought to be the most primitive known fossil scorpion, has been investigated with modern scanning techniques. Scans revealed the presence of book-lung internal structures and the investigators demonstrated that, though there is evidence for scorpions being terrestrial, there is absolutely no evidence for them having been aquatic.[7] The current specialist consensus is, therefore, that all scorpions – with one possible exception – were terrestrial.

The exception is *Waeringoscorpio*, which appears to have filamentous gill-like organs similar to those of some secondarily aquatic insects. These organs are thought to be a unique specialization of *Waeringoscorpio*, and are unlike eurypterid gills. It may therefore have been secondarily aquatic, unlike other early terrestrial scorpions. It remains probable that there was some relationship between the arachnid ancestor and eurypterids; however, the exact nature of this connection is unclear, particularly as we have yet to discover an example of an arachnid common ancestor.[8] Arachnids may have descended from eurypterids, or possibly had an ancestor in common with eurypterids, making them 'cousins' of sorts, although this has not been proven.

The fossil record for scorpions extends over numerous countries, including the United States, the United Kingdom, the Czech Republic and Russia. Scorpions have changed relatively little since their first appearance. As Dr Gess points out, scorpions can be viewed as a 'success story' – requiring relatively few new evolutionary adaptations over millions of years in order to flourish. The organization of their segments has remained mostly the same, unlike other creatures such as insects or crustaceans, who may have experienced 'fusing' of some segments. Due to the comparatively stagnant evolutionary aspect of scorpions, they were once thought of in science as 'living fossils'.[9] The fossils of terrestrial scorpions indicate that they coexisted with the first terrestrial tetrapods and are likely to have been preyed upon by them.

The scorpion's venom was an important survival tool which helped it, in turn, to catch its prey. A scientific study, published in *Molecular Biology and Evolution*, has shown that a single mutation in a protein that formed part of the scorpion's immune system was the origin of its venom.[10] At one point, the terrestrial scorpion ancestors had only a single means of prey capture – their pincer-like claws. This type of prey capture involved a great amount of risk, as grabbing and holding prey exposed them to potential injury. The most primitive and the largest of scorpions still have large claws and small tails, with mild venom. The more

Fossilized *Palaeophoneus nuncius*, the oldest-known genus of scorpion, discovered in Sweden.

evolutionarily advanced scorpions have the reverse: large tails and small claws. They traded mechanical means of catching prey for the ability to inflict a chemical-induced death.[11]

EARLY PERCEPTIONS AND ART

Now having looked at the earliest fossil records of scorpions, and considered their zoological origins, we move forwards in time to consider some of the early representations of scorpions in human thought and civilization. In 2013 Native American cave paintings were discovered in Tennessee – some over 6,000 years old.[12] The paintings are the oldest artworks to have been found in the United States, and among the drawings are pictures of scorpions. It is thought that the pictures show the cosmo-logical understanding of the world by prehistoric Native American settlers. Several animals are portrayed, including birds, human figures and dog-like creatures (canids). The draw-ings discovered in Tennessee are believed to represent the Native Americans' prehistoric world in three distinct dimensions – the upper parts of the depictions are 'celestial', representing reli-gious beliefs. The middle sections usually show plants, animals and the world in which they would have lived. Images in the lower parts of the caves and walls represents the lower world – a place of darkness and danger, with associations of death, renewal and transformation. Scorpions are represented as part of the Native Americans' 'lower world'; the drawings were found deep in the caves and not in the upper 'celestial' areas of the walls. Along with scorpions, other creatures depicted as associated with the lower world were supernatural serpents, dogs that accompan-ied dead humans on the path of souls and an 'earth spirit' who was involved in the making and unmaking of the world.[13] The ancient Native American drawings also show hybrid creatures,

Mesopotamian cylinder seal with a Scorpion Man.

which are part human and part animal, a concept explored in early Mesopotamian literature.

Gilgamesh is the world's oldest epic. Sumerian poems detailing the hero's adventures were probably first written around 2100 BCE, with the Standard Babylonian version, our focus here, dated to the first millenium BCE.[14] The legend comes from Mesopotamia, an ancient land known as the 'cradle of civilization' that geographically spanned modern-day Iraq, Kuwait, parts of Iran and areas of Syria and Turkey. The poem tells the story of Gilgamesh, the legendary king of the city of Uruk. *Enuma Elish* is the name of the Mesopotamian creation myth famous for its insights into the Babylonian cosmological worldview. The text of *Enuma Elish* is more than 1,000 lines in length, and takes its name from its opening lines, which can be translated as 'when on high'. In both of these early Mesopotamian epics, there are appearances in the text of the mysterious Scorpion Men.

The Scorpion Men are hybridized creatures with a distinctive appearance. Their upper bodies are human in form and they are bearded. Their lower bodies have the tail of a scorpion, the hindquarters and talons of a bird, and a serpent-headed penis. They are sometimes shown with wings. Many scholars believe that an earlier version of the Scorpion Man was a simpler hybrid of man and scorpion, without the reptile and bird features. A more accurate name for the Scorpion Men, which is also more in line with modern thought, would be 'Scorpion People', as the creatures can appear in female form. The Scorpion People are known to have a close and lasting bond with the Babylonian sun god Shamash. In the role of Shamash's attendants, the Scorpion People are often depicted in art standing below him and supporting a winged solar disc.

The ancient origins of the Scorpion Men are relayed in *Enuma Elish*. In it, they are one of eleven monster warriors created by the primordial goddess of the ocean, Tiamat, in her battle to avenge the death of the god of fresh water, Apsu. The creation of the Scorpion Men is listed in Tablet 1 of the epic, along with Tiamat's other monstrous creations:

> She [Tiamat] cloaked ferocious dragons with fearsome rays . . .
> She stationed a horned serpent . . . a rabid dog, a scorpion-man,
> Aggressive *umu*-demons, a fish-man, and a bull-man,
> Bearing merciless weapons, fearless in battle.
> Her orders were so powerful, they could not be disobeyed.[15]

In the myth, Tiamat is defeated by Marduk, a chief god who subsequently becomes the king of the Babylonian gods. The Scorpion Men and other creatures created by Tiamat are also subdued and domesticated, and they become benevolent forces, obliged to help humans and gods.[16] The Scorpion Men come to be guardians in the service of Shamash, and the image of a male and female pair of Scorpion People on figurines was thought to have an apotropaic, or protective, effect. It is in their capacity as guardians, and helpers of the gods, that the Scorpion People appear in the *Epic of Gilgamesh.*

Gilgamesh begins the poem as a tyrannical king, who is two-thirds divine and one-third mortal. His impetuous ways cause disharmony in the city of Uruk. To keep him busy, the gods create a wild-man companion, Enkidu, and after some initial friction the pair become devoted companions. They have several adventures together, including fighting the forest guardian Humbaba and the mighty Bull of Heaven. Through their bold actions, Gilgamesh and Enkidu insult the gods, however, which ultimately leads to the death of Enkidu. Devastated by the death of his friend, and fearing his own death in turn, Gilgamesh tries to find a way to live forever. Although two-thirds divine, Gilgamesh's humanity makes him completely mortal. To discover the means of attaining eternal life, Gilgamesh goes on a quest to find the only human who has gained this secret, Utnapishtim. In order to find him, Gilgamesh must travel along the path of the sun, underneath Mount Mashu. It is here that we find the Scorpion People, who guard the tunnel to the path of the sun. The Scorpion People are described as half human and half dragon, with terrifying glory and shimmering halos. They are able to recognize Gilgamesh's semi-divine nature, and grant him explicit permission to travel through Mount Mashu, a path never previously trod by any mortal. The Scorpion People warn Gilgamesh of the dangers of the path ahead, and then pronounce the gate of the mountain to be open.

The Scorpion People are presented as liminal creatures in the *Epic of Gilgamesh.* As well as inhabiting a space between human and animal, their role in the narrative is to guard the tunnel linking the sun, earth and sky. In the introduction of this book, it was noted that the potency of scorpions has been historically perceived as either protective or dangerous for humans. In the *Epic*, the

Scorpion People are presented as powerful creatures, and their presentation involves intriguing dualism. The Scorpion People are dangerous; with their death-striking glare, they cause even the heroic Gilgamesh to momentarily cover his eyes. At the same time, they are important guardians who are shown to be able to employ some autonomy and wisdom in their role as attendants of Shamash. In fact, the Scorpion Men are some of the few characters in the story who are capable of flexibility in their role. Although they guard the tunnel, they recognize Gilgamesh's heroic nature, and permit him to pass. Other fierce creatures encountered by Gilgamesh are destroyed by him, such as Humbaba the forest guardian, the Bull of Heaven and the lions near Mount Mashu. It is likely that the flexibility shown by the Scorpion Men in accommodating Gilgamesh helps them to avoid conflict. It is implied, also, that the cooperative nature of the Scorpion Men may be due to their liminality – their ability to exist in the nexus between different states of being seems to give them mysterious powers, wisdom and tractability. Alternatively, it is possible that the flexibility shown by the Scorpion Men has its basis in the ancient composers' observations of the adaptability of scorpions in the natural world. This interpretation fits well with the depiction of the Scorpion People's fierceness, which doubtless has its origins in the authors' recognition of the scorpion's animal power and occasionally aggressive behaviour.

While the depiction of Scorpion People shows some variation in different chronological periods of Mesopotamian history, what remains constant in their representation is their portrayal as benevolent helpers of the gods.[17] For the Mesopotamians, the divine harnessing of the dangerous powers of the scorpion allowed for that power to be utilized in a positive, protective manner.

SCORPION MEN BEYOND MESOPOTAMIA

The blending of two animal species, human and scorpion, to create a creature with magical, transgressive abilities is a mythological trope which extends beyond the Mesopotamian world. Scorpion Men can also be found in the myths of ancient Mesoamerica, a culture which extended from the American Southwest to Central America. Both the Aztec and Mayan civilizations had celestial bonds to scorpions, and both cultures shared the liminal creature in their mythology. In Aztec astrology, the Mesoamerican god of warfare and sacrifice took the form of a Scorpion Man.[18] The Scorpion Man in Mesoamerican tradition is often found as part of a male and female pair, as we have seen with the earlier Mesopotamian version of this character. The aggressive associations of scorpion imagery in this culture were not limited to astrology; the scorpion functioned as an emblem granted to a young warrior who had succeeded in successfully taking a captive for the first time.

Depictions of a giant scorpion monster are found in the Madrid Codex. This book is one of three surviving pre-Columbian

The Madrid Codex, one of three surviving pre-Columbian books of the Maya.

Mayan records, dating from around 900–1500 CE. In the Codex, the scorpion monster is depicted bringing forth rain from between its pincers. (The celestial aspect of scorpions in Meso-america will be further explored in Chapter Five.) Another famous hybrid monster with a scorpion feature is the legendary manticore. This beast originated in Persian myth, where it was called 'man-eater'. The manticore, with its human head, leonine body and scorpion's tail, was believed by many in the ancient world to be a real animal. The manticore's fame has proved enduring; it even received a mention in the third book in the *Harry Potter* series, as an example of a historical marauding beast.[19]

The Bible is full of vivid animal imagery, and scorpions appear in this ancient text in several places. It is difficult to be entirely sure exactly how many references to scorpions can be found in the Bible. A great deal of scholarly effort has been dedicated to defining which modern-day animals are being referred to by the ancient Hebrew names given for them in the Bible, and in the last 40 years new translations of the Bible and the influence of the Dead Sea Scrolls have greatly improved the accuracy of the assessment of the entomological content of the biblical text.[20] There is general agreement among biblical scholars that the word 'scorpion' (Hebrew *'aqrāb*) appears in the Old Testament in Deuteronomy 8:15 and Ezekiel 2:6; and in the New Testament (as the Greek *skorpios*) in Luke 10:19, 11:12 and Revelations 9:3, 5 and 10; and that these passages all refer to the scorpion animal, either literally (Deuteronomy 8:15, Luke 11:12) or symbolically (Ezekiel 2:6).[21] Scholarly opinion is divided over the remaining four mentions of the word 'scorpion', which occur in 1 Kings 12:11 and 14 and 2 Chronicles 10:11 and 14. With these four mentions of the Hebrew word for 'scorpion', it is very difficult to ascertain whether an animal or a type of weapon is referred to.

One mention of scorpions is found in Deuteronomy 8:14–15:

> You forget the Lord your God, who brought you out of the land of Egypt, out of the house of bondage, who led you through the great and terrible wilderness, with its fiery serpents and scorpions and thirsty ground where there was no water, who brought you water out of the flinty ground.

In these two verses from Deuteronomy, scorpions are presented negatively, and as a natural hazard. The coupling of the 'fiery' serpents and scorpions and the dry ground in this passage suggests that the choice of scorpion imagery here may be an indication of their reputation for being a particular hazard of a wild desert environment.

> And now, whereas my father laid upon you a heavy yoke,
> I will add to your yoke. My father chastised you with whips,
> but I will chastise you with scorpions. (1 Kings 12:11)

The above sentiments are repeated almost identically in 1 Kings 12:14 and in 2 Chronicles 10:11 and 14, with all attributed to King Rehoboam. Several scholars suggest that the word used for 'scorpion' here may be a reference to a type of weapon, such as a type of whip armed with sharp end-points to make the lash more severe, although this view is not universally accepted.[22] Other scholars (perhaps wisely) sidestep the issue entirely.[23] Contextually, the weapon interpretation appears most plausible. King Rehoboam is speaking of a man-made device for punishment, the yoke, and then says he will add to this yoke. Through the use of parallelism, a pattern to his speech is set up where an existing punishment is intensified while remaining essentially the same. Following this is the promise that the punishment by whips will be replaced by scorpions; a 'scorpion' lash is known to have existed in Roman times, but whether such a weapon had this name in Old Testament times is uncertain. Further, it is Rehoboam speaking in these instances, not God, and throughout the Bible only God is shown to have power over the scorpion animal. In either case, the presentation of the scorpion in these four verses is not positive – the animal either has a sting more painful than the lash of a whip, or provides a particularly nasty whip with its name.

Scorpion depicted on a 13th-century parchment.

We move swiftly along from this controversy to the next mention of scorpions in the Bible, found in Ezekiel 2:6. This reference

iiille. Et leo sunt ge[ner]i incendib[us] nasc[itur] sp[er]entiu[m] uir[?] munita sol[um] ad mor[t]s h[?]mm[?]u t[?]
tib[us]. Deniq[ue] imp[?] natos p[ar]uulos sp[er]cib[us] t[er]ricdos dilac[er]at q[?] si togenes cetur[?] [?] addicto o[?]
cep[?] g[ra]tuito n[?]cebat[ur] sm[?]u cet[ur] g[e]niosi t[?] led[?]bat[?]. Ij g[en]s st[?]r z[?] c[?] q[uia] anat[?]m[?]b[?] de
lat[?]
est.

hos pedes fissule q[uia] a[?]mins vero co[?]p[?] h[?]sp[?]de
[?]uolam[ur].

fornice magno q[ue] au[?]
ans seruant h[?]rnas.

seorp

occurs in the context of reported speech from a vision of God to the prophet Ezekiel, where he is commanded to address the people of Israel:

> And you, son of man, be not afraid of them, nor be afraid of their words, though briers and thorns are with you and you sit upon scorpions; be not afraid of their words, nor be dismayed at their looks, for they are a rebellious house.

Three of the references to scorpions in the New Testament occur in the space of eight verses in the Book of Revelation, as part of an apocalyptic vision:

> Then from the smoke came locusts on the earth, and they were given power like the power of scorpions on the earth; they were told not to harm the grass of the earth or any green growth of any tree, but only those of mankind who have not the seal of God on their foreheads; they were allowed to torture them for five months, but not to kill them, and their torture was like the torture of a scorpion when it stings a man. (Revelation 9:3–5)

There are also two further references to scorpions in the New Testament, in the Gospel of Luke:

> Behold, I give unto you power to tread on serpents and scorpions, and over all the power of the enemy: and nothing shall by any means hurt you. (Luke 10:19)

> And I tell you: Ask, and it will be given; seek, and you will find; knock and it will be opened to you. For everyone who asks receives, and he who seeks finds, and to him who

knocks it will be opened. What father among you, if his son asks for a fish, will instead of a fish give him a serpent; or if he asks for an egg, will give him a scorpion? (Luke 11:9–12)

These references to scorpions from the New Testament conform to the pattern that has been observed here for the usage of scorpion imagery in the ancient world – all but one acknowledge the natural power of the scorpion, with Luke 11:9–12 being a possible exception to this rule. While in Luke 11 the scorpion is compared to the serpent – which is also often portrayed as having 'dangerous power' in biblical texts – both scorpion and serpent are contrasted with fish and eggs, through the passage's use of parallelism. The eggs and fish are referred to as 'good' things to give to children. Context would suggest that there is an ethical element to the mention of scorpions. The next line following the scorpion reference is moral in tone:

If you then, who are evil, know how to give good gifts to your children, how much more will the heavenly Father give the Holy Spirit to those who ask him! (Luke 11:13)

It seems the contrast in Luke 11 is not only between edible and inedible things, but between edible 'good' things and dangerous things that are most likely inedible, or between good parenting and parenting which leads to envenomation. The passage's focus on paternal care would mean the scorpion is presented as an inappropriately hazardous gift for a child (as a snake might be).[24]

Although we shall see in a later chapter that scorpions are viewed by many people as a source of food, from a biblical perspective it seems probable that they are prohibited from consumption. Snakes and scorpions could have been included in the list of unclean foods from Leviticus 11:41–2:

Every swarming thing that swarms upon the earth is an abomination, it shall not be eaten. Whatever goes on its belly, and whatever goes on all fours, or whatever has many feet, all the swarming things that swarm upon the earth, you shall not eat; for they are an abomination.

While scorpions are not specifically listed, due to the fairly vague descriptions of crawling things in Leviticus, most (but not all) such creatures have been generally considered to be unclean.[25]

We can therefore tentatively say that all direct references to scorpions in the Bible display an awareness of the animal's natural power, and scorpions in the Bible are presented in a uniformly negative light. While the scorpion is depicted as dangerous, powerful and capable of inflicting pain, its potency is shown to be insignificant next to the power of God. Humans are shown to be at risk from the power of the scorpion, but can be protected by God. The clear hierarchy in the text, where God's power is superior to that of the scorpions, is shown in Deuteronomy 8:14–15. God is shown in this passage to have authority over naturally dangerous elements, such as fiery serpents and drought, which would otherwise be harmful to the Israelites. Scorpions are presented in the passage as another dangerous environmental element under God's control. The hierarchy is further elucidated through the words of Jesus in Luke 10:19, where 70 of Jesus' followers are assured of their safety from dangerous yet powerful enemies.

The Assyrian King Sargon II with a dignitary, from a wall relief at the palace of Sargon II at Dur-Sharrukin (the Assyrian empire's capital, now Khorsabad in Iraq).

THE SCORPION QUEEN

It is important to note an ancient connection between royalty and scorpion imagery that is found in ancient Mesopotamia. While in ancient Egypt the connection between monarch and scorpion

74

A bloodstone (jasper) scorpion ring set in gold.

Scorpion ring.

was predominately masculine, in Mesopotamia we find evidence of a Scorpion Queen (in Mesopotamia, the king was closely associated with imagery of lions and bulls). Evidence from Assur and royal tombs in Nimrud have shown the association of Assyrian queens with scorpions. The scorpion can be seen as a royal symbol, used to signify the queen and also the royal harem. One monarchic example of this is Atalia, the queen of Sargon II (721–705 BCE), who had pictures of scorpions incised on a gold bowl and a mirror.[26] Items containing a scorpion seal are believed to be related to the administration of royal women's properties and residences.

Scorpions in Mesopotamia were associated with fertility (often being depicted alongside images of the Tree of Life), and their imagery bore religious significance. The Mesopotamian goddess of love and battle, Ishtar (known in Sumerian as Inanna), was closely connected to scorpions. Inanna is the earliest goddess for which we have written evidence. She is known for her highly ambitious nature, which is frequently a key narrative device in her myths. A little-known text featuring Inanna shows the goddess attempting to gain control of the heavens, formerly the dominion of the sky god, An. The goddess must overcome several protective creatures in her attempt to storm the heavens – including a scorpion. Inanna defeats the scorpion by stamping on it, then rips off the creature's tail, an action that causes the animal to bellow like a lion. While the translation of this ancient text is extremely fragmentary, there is a possible reference to the goddess then securing the tail upon her own body. This text (known as *Inanna and An*) may be the first written account of a scorpion in mythology, and we can see that the scorpion is presented as a powerful, protective creature, employed as a guardian of the heavens. The locus of the scorpion's power in the myth is in its tail, which is why the goddess must remove this part of the creature's anatomy. The goddess's ability to overcome the potent animal enhances her prestige, and the story ends in her praise.

The appearance of the scorpion emblem on items connected to or belonging to women in Assyrian archaeological remains suggests that pictures of scorpions were a gender signifier, relating to the specific worship carried out by women.[27] The usage of

Peter Paul Rubens,
The Head of Medusa,
c. 1617–18,
oil on canvas
(detail).

scorpion symbolism had erotic associations, and it is possible that the scorpion's intimate association with women as well as the goddess of sex may have signified the power of women's sexuality over men.[28] This connection may have been inspired by the observation of the female scorpion's occasional consumption of her male lover after mating.

The use of scorpion symbolism in the ancient Near East shows intriguing variety. While Mesopotamian and Egyptian goddesses were associated with scorpions in myth and iconography, a remarkable divide along gender lines can also be observed for the deployment of this symbolism in connection to kings and queens. Why is the scorpion emblematic of the Assyrian queen? It appears the most likely answer to this question has been given by Karen Radner, who suggests that the scorpion's reputation as a protective mother may have seemed a fitting mascot for a queen whose role was to give birth to a crown prince, and to protect and support him in his ascent to rulership.[29] The association of the power of the scorpion with positive maternal qualities will be further explored in the following chapter.

The natural power of the scorpion has been recognized in ancient times by many diverse cultures. The negative portrayal of scorpions in the Bible as dangerous and undesirable (and most likely inedible) creatures has likely influenced the way scorpions are perceived in the modern age. In the Bible, the dangerous aspect of the scorpion dominates its image, and this identification continues in modern artistic culture, seemingly outlasting the more protective aspects of scorpion imagery seen in Mesopotamian culture and royal symbolism.

3 The Scorpion King

He who has been stung by a scorpion
lives afraid of even its shadow.
Spanish proverb

Egypt is home to two main families of scorpion – the darker and fairly harmless Scorpionidae, and the lighter-coloured, extremely dangerous Buthidae.[1] The effect on Egyptian thought of the awareness of the potency of the latter type can be seen in the scorpion's powerful role in Egyptian kingship and divinity. The scorpion has ancient ties to royalty in Egypt, where the creature also featured prominently in myth and magic. Two Egyptian goddesses were associated with scorpions – the goddess Serket, who is thought to have originated as a deified scorpion, and the well-known mother-goddess Isis. The close connection of Isis with Egyptian kingship makes her association with scorpions especially significant.

The fierceness of the scorpion has been shown at times to have a positive, protective association in ancient Egypt. This positive image is seen alongside more dangerous depictions of the scorpion in Egyptian myths and magic, revealing the complexity of the ancient Egyptians' conceptualization of the scorpion. The juxtaposition of positive characteristics alongside dangerous and menacing ones in portrayals of the scorpion has been carried through to the modern age, with the portrayal of the 'Scorpion King' first as a dangerous villain and then as the heroic protagonist in the films of the *Scorpion King* series.

The conceptualization of animal figures symbolizing the attributes of a king occurs very early in ancient Egyptian history, with the image of the scorpion among the first recorded examples. Late Predynastic 'slate' palettes show conquering figures, perhaps representative of a king, depicted in animal forms (a bull, a lion and a scorpion). Amarna historian Barry J. Kemp suggests that this development in Egyptian history focuses intellectual and organizational efforts on projecting kingship as the symbol of supreme power over others. The Narmer Palette and mace heads, and the Scorpion Mace Head, build on this representation of royal imagery by including the earliest-known depictions of an Egyptian king. These materials were discovered at Hierakonpolis (Falcon City), which was the political and religious capital of Upper

The home of tomb U-J, burial place of the ancient ruler Scorpion, at the Temple at Abydos, Egypt.

Limestone mace head of the Scorpion King carved in low relief.

Egypt during the Predynastic Period (*c.* 4500–3100 BCE) and most likely the early Protodynastic Period (3100–2686 BCE). Images of lions and bulls were also closely connected to kingship in ancient Egypt, as well as in the nearby region of Mesopotamia.[2] In 1898 the British archaeologists Frederick W. Green and James E. Quibell discovered the Scorpion King Mace Head while working at Hierakonpolis, about 600 km (373 miles) south of Cairo. The important finds from the expedition were divided between the Cairo Museum and the Ashmolean Museum of the University of Oxford, where the Mace Head is now exhibited. The Scorpion King Mace Head is five times the size of a traditional mace head, which suggests ceremonial rather than practical usage. It depicts a ruler wearing the White Crown of Upper (southern) Egypt and performing an aspect of a ceremony connected with opening an irrigation channel or laying a foundation trench. In front of his

Detail of the Scorpion King on the mace head.

face is a scorpion emblem. It is thought that this emblem is a hieroglyph of the king's name, and is one of the earliest examples of hieroglyphic writing discovered to date.[3]

The identity of the early pharaohs Scorpion I and II have been disputed in modern scholarship, and their exact chronological placement among Egypt's early rulers is uncertain. Quibell was the first in the field to use the term 'Dynasty 0' to describe the artefacts found at Hierakonpolis which preceded the first Egyptian dynasties. Although evidence for this Predynastic Period is scarce, it was doubtlessly a formative time for Egypt. Next to nothing is known of King Scorpion, although it is probable that he was a historical ruler whose reign occurred prior to that of King Narmer.[4] A commonly held view is that the Scorpion Mace

Head depicts an early king, Scorpion II, a southern ruler who took steps towards conquering the northern kingdom and finally creating a union between the two lands of Egypt. This process was then consolidated by King Narmer.[5] On the Scorpion Narmer Palette, the Egyptian king is seen destroying many cities in the Nile Delta, and is depicted as a lion and a falcon. Between the end of the Predynastic Period and later times, there was a marked change in the symbolism of animals. Scorpions (along with catfish) were prominent royal symbols in the Predynastic Period but ceased to be later on, although the reasons for this ideological change are unknown.[6]

Despite its small proportions, the scorpion is capable of delivering a fatal blow with a single strike of its tail, to opponents more than 100 times its size – a feat only comparable in efficiency to some species of snake and spider. Combined with its extreme toughness and adaptability, the scorpion makes a formidable opponent. The observation of the scorpion's strength as a combatant is a likely cause for its popularity in the royal ideology of the

The ancient Egyptian Narmer Palette, from Hierakonpolis.

warrior kings of the ancient Near East. Scorpions are widespread in Egypt in the low desert, which is also the habitat of wild hunting dogs. They, too, were powerful symbols of the late Predynastic Period, though not thought to be related to kingship.

THE SCORPION AND THE GODDESS

In addition to being related to early kingship in ancient Egypt, the scorpion had a lasting association with the Egyptian gods. This duality in the scorpion's role is perhaps to be expected, as kingship and religion were tightly interwoven in ancient Egyptian ideology. The exact definition of the divinity of Egyptian kings has been a source of debate in recent times. Initially, research on the issue was focused on the divine elements of the Pharaoh, to the near exclusion of more human qualities.[7] In more recent studies, the less divine, more human elements of the king have become the focus of investigation, to the extent that questions have been raised as to whether the divinity of the Egyptian king was rooted in the office or person of Pharaoh.[8] Nonetheless, the Egyptians considered their kings to be of divine birth, and while the living Pharaoh was identified with the god Horus, in death the king became associated with Osiris. The name Horus means 'the distant one' or 'the one on high', while Osiris is a Greek rendering of the Egyptian *Usir*. The meaning of *Usir* is uncertain, but a possible interpretation of the hieroglyphic symbols is 'Place of the Eye'. A common epithet of Osiris is 'Foremost of the Westerners', a name referring to his role as the dead king.

It has been noted above that the scorpion's strength could connote protection as well as combat in ancient Egypt. While the link between kingship and the scorpion seems likely to have had its genesis in the appreciation of the scorpion as a dangerous combatant, in religion the emphasis seems to be on its protective

Ankh-auf-Mut adoring a seated Osiris, Egyptian, 11th Dynasty, painting on wood.

nature. This protective element is seen in Egyptian myth, religion, medicine and magic, and particularly with two goddesses: Serket and Isis.

The goddess Serket was originally a deified scorpion, and she is depicted as a woman wearing a headdress in the form of a scorpion with its sting raised. Her skill lay in healing poisonous stings and bites. The name 'Serket' means 'she who tightens the throat' – a reference to the asphyxiating paralysis caused by a scorpion's sting. Serket's name could also mean 'she who causes the throat to breathe' – expressing the healing aspect of the goddess, along with the inherent duality found in the conceptualization of scorpions in Egyptian culture. Through her association with medicine and healing magic, physicians were given the title 'follower of Serket', or 'one who wields power over the goddess Serket' (or 'is powerful over Serket's venom'). Servants of Serket and the lion-headed goddess Sekhmet worked alongside physicians in Egypt's mines, quarries and building sites.[9] Their sacerdotal expertise included medical prescriptions and magical spells to treat scorpion stings.[10]

The connection of Serket and her followers to the protection of the king has ancient origins, and from the middle of the third millennium BCE Serket was depicted protecting the throne of the king in the guise of a scorpion.[11] The scorpion goddess was also a protector of the dead, and her image is frequently seen on canopic jars, in particular the jar containing the intestine. Serket's power over poisonous creatures and serpents meant she was an important deity in combating the Egyptian god of darkness and chaos, Apophis. The serpentine Apophis was an evil god opposed to the Egyptian concept of *Ma'at* (truth, law, order). Apophis frequently battled the sun god, Ra, who was later merged with Horus to become Re-Horakhty ('Ra, who is Horus of the Two Horizons'). Serket was an important defender of Ra in his battles

against Apophis, and her power over reptiles meant she could grasp Apophis' serpentine tail. When Apophis was imprisoned, Serket would guard and restrain him from escaping. One of the most famous depictions of Serket is found on the outer sarcophagus of Tutankhamun. Along with Isis, Nephthys and Neith, Serket is depicted protecting the body of the king.

The image of Serket was at times conflated with that of the Egyptian mother goddess, Isis – one of the most prominent of the Egyptian gods. Isis is the devoted wife of Osiris and protective mother of Horus – and so she is intimately linked to both the living and dead king. Serket protected both the living king, and the body and viscera of the dead, perhaps suggesting a liminal quality to the Egyptian conception of goddesses linked to scorpion imagery.

The meaning of the name 'Isis' is unclear, but it has associations with a seat or throne, and this hieroglyphic symbol is used

Statue of Serket protecting Tutankhamun's shrine. The goddess's emblem, a scorpion, sits upon her head.

in the writing of her name. It has been suggested by the noted Egyptologist Henri Frankfort that Isis was originally personified as the deified throne upon which the king of Egypt was seated.[12] In this way, Isis makes the king the ruler of Egypt, as it is through his mother (the throne) that the king is raised to rule – more literally than figuratively. It is very difficult to know if the Egyptians actually conceived of the relationship between the king and Isis in this way, but the goddess's connection to the throne cannot be doubted.

The first known written appearance of Isis is in the Pyramid Texts. These sacred texts were carved on the walls of the pyramids of King Wenis of the end of the Fifth Dynasty and the rulers of the Sixth Dynasty. The Pyramid Texts are notoriously difficult to accurately date, as they are thought to contain a mixture of materials contemporaneous with the pyramids in which they are inscribed, alongside much more ancient material. In the texts, Isis takes a very proactive and independent role in protecting her son Horus from his morally questionable uncle, Seth. In these myths, we can observe the close interplay of scorpions, kingship, divinity and motherhood in ancient Egyptian thought. In the Osiris–Horus–Isis cycle of myths, Isis is left to raise and guard Horus after Osiris is murdered by his scheming brother, Seth. Isis must repeatedly outwit Seth to prevent him from killing or otherwise interfering with her son. It is intriguing to wonder whether the apparent link between scorpions, protective mothers and kings seen in Egyptian myth had its origins in observations of the natural world. As discussed in the chapter on biology, scorpion mothers often carry their newborn babies safely on their backs.

An important myth involving Isis illustrates the protective connection between mother, scorpion and young king. The myth is called *Isis and the Seven Scorpions.* The story begins with Isis, the loyal wife, weaving the linen wrappings for the mummy of her dead husband, Osiris. Thoth, the ibis-headed Egyptian god of wisdom, visits her to warn that she must take her young son Horus into hiding to protect him from his uncle Seth. Isis takes Thoth's warning seriously, and that evening sets off with Horus, to be accompanied by a guard of seven scorpions. Three of the scorpions – Tjetet, Petet and Matet – preceded her and ascertained that the path ahead was safe. By her side were two more scorpions, Mesetet and Mesetetef. Following the small party were Tefen and Befen. Every night, Isis warned her scuttling companions to be very mindful of not alerting Seth to where she was. She instructed the scorpions not to speak to any strangers they met along the way. One night, as Isis was travelling through the

Nile Delta, she arrived at a town called the Two Sisters. In the place of a welcome from the town's wealthy family, Isis had the door slammed in her face by the lady of the house. The scorpions were enraged at the woman's treatment of their mistress and the neglect of the customs of hospitality. The scorpions set their hearts on vengeance. In preparation, six of the scorpions added their personal poisons to Tefen, who loaded his stinger with it. Meanwhile, a humble peasant girl offered her simple home as a refuge to Isis. Bristling with poison, Tefen snuck out of the house. Stealthily, he crawled under the door of the noblewoman's house and stung her son. Seeing her son almost at the point of death from the scorpion's sting, the wealthy lady ran through the town, desperately seeking assistance – but no one could help her. The cries of the wealthy lady reached Isis, who by nature was very forgiving. Despite the noblewoman's uncharitable behaviour towards her, Isis would not allow the death of an innocent child where she could help. So, the goddess returned to the woman's home to help her son. Isis held the little boy in her arms, while speaking powerful incantations of great magic. She named each of the scorpions, which gave her control over them and caused their poisons to become harmless to the child. The noblewoman was humbled by Isis' kindness and forgiving nature. She offered all of her wealth to Isis and to the humble peasant girl who had shown hospitality to a stranger. This myth shows the complexity of the Egyptian's conception of the scorpion. The scorpions in the myth show the now familiar behaviours of being fierce opponents and vigilant guards, but there is a moral element involved that seems to govern whether they are protective or destructive. Kind and loyal Isis is protected by the scorpions, and the peasant girl has nothing to fear from them. For the wrongdoer, however, the scorpions prepare a formidable punishment. The scorpions' punishment is targeted not on the woman's life, but on her identity

Detail of side panels from the trough of a painted wooden coffin showing a chapter from *The Book of the Dead*. The scorpions held by serpents likely represent the dead calling upon Serket for protection from the animal's deadly sting.

as a mother – in contrast to the protection they give to Isis in her maternal role.

Myths involving Isis and scorpions may have been ritually acted out in festivals known from Roman times, where members of the cult of Isis would handle live scorpions, and the goddess was invoked in Egyptian magic to cure scorpion stings.[13] The protective mother-goddess Taweret was also magically invoked in the treatment of scorpionism. Taweret was thought to protect women in childbirth and was the Egyptian goddess of fertility; her name means 'Great One'. She is depicted as a pregnant hippopotamus with the legs and arms of a lion, the tail of a crocodile and a woman's breasts. Taweret was linked protectively to Horus, and perhaps for this reason was invoked on the behalf of children suffering from scorpion stings.[14] Again, we see the convergence of Egyptian goddesses who are associated with scorpions providing protection to the king.

It should be noted that scorpions have been associated with goddesses – especially mother-goddesses – outside of Egyptian culture as well. The Nicaraguan creator deity, Itoki, is called

'Great Mother', and is conceptualized as a mother scorpion who lives at the edge of the Milky Way. She is thought to send the new souls of those newly born to their human life, and, like Serket, she has a role in receiving the souls of those who have recently died.[15] A goddess from the Nahua culture of central Mexico, Xochiquetzal, was invoked to cure the sting of scorpions and, like Taweret, protected women in childbirth.[16]

A duality can be seen in the role of scorpions in ancient Egyptian medicine and magic. Scorpions were inscribed on amulets for protection, and Serket was invoked in Egyptian magic to cure venomous bites. At the same time, many spells have been found which are focused on driving scorpions away and preventing them from stinging, or preparing a magical barrier at the threshold of a dwelling to bar venomous creatures from entry. The most famous depictions of scorpions in ancient Egypt, known as 'Horus Cippi', are directly associated with the king, and these stelae were used to protect Egyptian people from dangerous animals. These protective stelae show Horus, as a child, standing on two crocodiles and holding scorpions, a horned creature and a lion. When a talisman containing these images was placed in a house, it meant that the house was under the protection of Horus and his companion gods and goddesses, who had vanquished all the hosts of darkness and all the physical and moral forces of evil.[17]

HORUS AND THE SCORPION

We have seen that scorpions, in Egyptian myth, played an important role in protecting young Horus from Seth, and also that the child Horus seems to play an important role protecting others *against* scorpions. Another Egyptian myth, however, of Horus and the Scorpion, contains a less heroic role for the scorpion. In this, Isis has hidden Horus in the marshes of Akh-bit (Khemmis) in the Nile Delta, and left him in order to find food for herself. When she returns to the hiding place, she finds that Horus had been stung by a scorpion. Although in the myth of the seven scorpions the magic of Isis effectively counteracted the scorpions' venom, Isis in this myth becomes greatly distressed and is unable to help Horus. Her screams attract the attention of the sun god, Ra, who reacts quickly. He brings his solar boat to a halt in its journey across the sky, causing the whole land to be plunged into darkness. The wise god Thoth disembarks from Ra's boat and incants a spell to cure Horus of his sting. Thoth threatens that the earth will remain in darkness until the poison leaves Horus' body. Horus is healed by Thoth's magic and restored to health. Thoth then

Horus the child and scorpions, standing on crocodiles, Egyptian 30th Dynasty, c. 380–343 BCE.

leaves the people of Akh-bit with the duty of caring for Horus, and returns to the solar boat, which continues on its celestial voyage. Although scorpions are a danger to Horus in this myth, in other sources his hiding place is protected by the scorpion goddess Serket.[18] Once again, we see the juxtaposition of the combative and protective aspects of the scorpion in Egyptian thought.

THE SCORPION KING IN FILM: *THE MUMMY RETURNS*

Despite the fact that very little evidence remains to inform us about the early Egyptian kings Scorpion I and Scorpion II, a successful film franchise has been made with the lead character's epithet 'The Scorpion King' referring to the historical Scorpion II. Although *The Mummy* and *Scorpion King* franchises are focused on providing lively entertainment rather than strict historical accuracy, the choices of imagery and myth utilized by the film-makers frequently show thoughtfulness and sophistication.

The character of the Scorpion King, played by Dwayne 'The Rock' Johnson, first appears in the film *The Mummy Returns* (2001), a sequel to the successful remake of *The Mummy* (1999). The film's opening scenes generate a fresh mythological background to the king's association with scorpions. They show a large army in Thebes, 3067 BCE, carrying standards into battle bearing the image of a golden scorpion. Thebes is perhaps most famous for its role as the Egyptian capital throughout most of the Eighteenth Dynasty, with the exception of the reigning period of Akhenaton. The film's Scorpion King is introduced by voice-over as a great king who aimed to rule over the whole world, perhaps showing some interplay by the film's writers with the historical King Scorpion II's own empire-building.

The Scorpion King carries a large shield with a scorpion painted on it, as well as a golden scorpion breastplate. Completing his armour is an item that is referenced in the film as 'the Bracelet of Anubis' – a golden bracelet carrying the image of a scorpion with its stinger raised and ready to strike. Despite the lead actor's impressive pedigree from WWE (World Wrestling Entertainment), the Scorpion King's army are defeated after a seven-year battle, and vanquished into the desert of Ahm Shere. After the rest of his army succumbs to the desert's harsh environmental conditions, the Scorpion King makes a deal with the jackal-headed Egyptian god Anubis. The association of Anubis with embalming and the afterlife makes him in many ways a good fit for the cinematic mythology of *The Mummy Returns*, with its heavy focus on revivified mummies as villains, but additionally there is some ancient evidence potentially linking Anubis with scorpions. Anubis may have been called upon, with Isis, in Egyptian spells used for the magical healing of scorpion stings. The evidence for this is found in the Leyden Papyrus, which is closely related to Greek Magical Papyri – a collection of spells, hymns and rituals that were preserved in Graeco-Roman Egypt. These texts were the result of attempts to preserve some of the magical heritage of the ancient world at a time when the use of magic was suppressed. It is thought that several Roman emperors tried to extirpate magic and divination because they recognized how it could grant the practitioner power and knowledge.[19] The suppression of magic resulted in the systematic destruction of magical texts – according to the Roman historian Suetonius (70–130 CE), the Roman emperor Augustus ordered 2,000 magical scrolls to be burned in the year 13 BCE.[20] In the Leyden Papyrus, there is the following spell, which is thought to be magically directed against the sting of a scorpion:

Spell to be said to the sting. 'I am the king's son, greatest and first, Anubis. My mother Sekhmet-Isis comes after me . . . saying "Hurry, hurry! Quickly, quickly, my child, king's son, greatest and first, Anubis," saying "Arise and come to Egypt, for your father Osiris is King of Egypt" . . . She coiled, and she came to me with a sting; I sat down and I wept. Isis, my mother, sat near me, saying to me "Do not weep, do not weep, my child, king's son, greatest and first, Anubis! Lick from your tongue to your heart, and vice versa, as far as the edges of the wound.'"[21]

In the film, the Scorpion King exchanges his soul for Anubis's aid in destroying his enemies. Once the warriors of Anubis have completed the Scorpion King's conquest, his soul is claimed by the jackal-headed god. Although he is one of the main villains of the film, the Scorpion King is mainly absent from the action of *The Mummy Returns*. The character only returns in the climax, which is staged in his hidden pyramid lair (crowned with a scorpion sculpture at its peak). The palace-like interior of the pyramid is decorated with scorpion imagery – there is an enormous sculpture of a scorpion in the throne room, and images of giant scorpions adorn the walls and pillars. Scorpion paintings even cover the floor, and one particularly useful set of wall paintings shows the protagonists a step-by-step approach to killing the Scorpion King. (In the DVD commentary, the writer and director Stephen Sommers and executive producer Bob Ducsay have an amusing and light-hearted discussion on the impracticalities of decorating a home with a mural predicting one's own doom.)

The Scorpion King is finally summoned from the Underworld by the series' main villain, Imhotep, who beats a giant gong adorned with – what else? – a scorpion. The physical appearance of the Scorpion King has been greatly transformed from the film's opening scenes; he has become a huge monster that is half-scorpion and half-man. The metamorphosis into this creature makes the Scorpion King a more dangerous combatant, one who can rip apart a victim with his oversized claws. In his hybridized state, he is almost invulnerable, perhaps in acknowledgement of the scorpion's legendary toughness.

However, the character does show limited vulnerability to fire when a jar of flaming liquid is tipped over him. The combination of a scorpion and flames is reminiscent of the urban myth that a scorpion, surrounded by flames and with no hope of escape, will sting itself to death. While there have been several eyewitness accounts of scorpions self-destructing, generally this myth is not considered to be based on biological reality. According to the Discovery Centre of the Museum Victoria, in Melbourne, a scorpion, like other animals, will panic if confronted with fire and will thrash its tail wildly[22] – much as the Scorpion King does when faced with fire in *The Mummy Returns*. Even with his giant size and arachnid toughness, the Scorpion King is finally killed after being stabbed with a mystical weapon: the Spear of Osiris. The film-makers' choice of myth is again nuanced and interesting: the Scorpion King's power in the film comes from Anubis, but he is destroyed by an artefact related to Osiris – perhaps playing on Osiris' replacement of Anubis as Lord of the Underworld in Egyptian mythology.

THE *SCORPION KING* FRANCHISE

In *The Mummy Returns*, the Scorpion King is a dangerous, morally ambiguous enemy to the series' protagonists. This first cinematic portrayal of the character can be contrasted with the more heroic and morally defined characterization in subsequent films. The events of *The Scorpion King* (2002) precede those of *The Mummy Returns*, and the film tells the story of Mathayus and his rise to become the Scorpion King. Mathayus is the last of the Akkadians, an empire of ancient Mesopotamia that was arguably the world's

The heroes Rick and Evelyn in *The Mummy Returns* (2001).

first great empire.[23] The knowledge of very early cultural contact and exchange between the ancient Egyptians and Mesopotamians creates an intriguing cinematic context for the story of one of Egypt's first empire-builders. Mathayus starts the film as a mercenary, hired to kill the sorceress of the invading warrior king, Memnon. While first motivated by economic concerns, Mathayus is soon compelled to fight for revenge against the ruthless Memnon, who murders Mathayus' brother Jesup. Mathayus survives poisoning from an arrow laced with scorpion venom, and is healed by the sorceress Cassandra. The sorceress tells our hero of a prophecy – that when the moon reaches the House of Scorpio, the great king will become the Scorpion King. She also warns him that facing Memnon will probably lead to his death – to which Mathayus responds that he will make his own destiny. With the aid of his companions, including a Nubian king and a horse thief, Mathayus is able to kill Memnon in his fortress and fulfil the prophecy, becoming the titular Scorpion King. The sorceress again warns that the period of peace may not last forever, and Mathayus once more assures her that he will make his own destiny.

Mathayus' motivation of revenge in *The Scorpion King* is a recurring motif that provides a sense of unity to his characterization in the *The Mummy Returns* and the first two *Scorpion King* films. In the *Scorpion King*'s sequel, *The Scorpion King 2: Rise of a Warrior* (2008), Mathayus attempts to get revenge on the legendary King of Akkad, Sargon, following the death of Mathayus' father. Mathayus joins Sargon's Black Scorpion squad, and is marked with a scorpion tattoo. This third film to feature the Scorpion King contains a bewildering array of mythical elements, which have been blended in service of the plot from greatly divergent time periods and cultural contexts. Again, the focus of the films is more

The Scorpion King in battle, in *The Scorpion King* (2002).

weighted towards entertainment than education, but the film seems slightly less dexterous in its incorporation of the historical and mythical elements that had provided depth to the earlier films. However, there is an interesting interplay created in the film between King Sargon and scorpions. In the climax of the film, Sargon transforms into a giant scorpion in order to battle with Mathayus. As discussed in the previous chapter, the scorpion was a favoured motif of the female members of the royal court of Sargon II. While Sargon himself was identified with lions and bulls, the queen and the royal harem were associated with scorpions.[24]

The most recently released film of the franchise, *The Scorpion King 3: Battle for Redemption* (2012), is more in line with the earlier films in its subtle and thoughtful means of employing mythical ideology. The main narrative is focused on Mathayus' efforts to unite Egypt, a role we associate with the historical Scorpion King. Mathayus' motivation is less about revenge, and more about creating a lasting legacy. The Scorpion King's enemies use the *Book of the Dead*, which is an interesting choice as scorpions appear several times in the Egyptian *Book of the Dead*. In the chapter for the prevention of dying, scorpions are again named as a curse on the enemies of the deceased, with the command that the scorpion should be on the enemies' bones. Scorpions also appear in the *Book of the Dead* in the spell for being transformed into a swallow, where the speaker aligns himself with the (unnamed) scorpion goddess. A further addition to the *Scorpion King* franchise, *The Scorpion King: Quest for Power*, was released in 2015.

In the cinematic character of the Scorpion King, we can see a reflection of the complexity and dualism present in the ancient Egyptians' conceptualization of scorpions in the areas of kingship, religion and myth. The Scorpion King is a daring combatant, showing the dangerous animal power associated with the scorpion, and its use in royal ideology. His appearance in *The Mummy Returns* shows the unpredictable nature of that animal power, as he is an enemy to the heroes of the series, but then becomes the hero of his own *Scorpion King* franchise. In this franchise, we can see a moral element to the Scorpion King's characterization, in his focus on vengeance. Further, the role of the historical Scorpion King as an empire-builder is referenced in *The Mummy Returns* and *The Scorpion King 3: Battle for Redemption*.

The association of scorpion symbolism with ancient Egyptian kingship seems perfectly suited to the image of the animal's emblematic guarding and attacking behaviour. Two key items of Egyptian royal regalia are the crook and the flail, which closely align with the protective reputation of the scorpion, and the 'sting' of its attack.[25] These two items of royal iconography evoke the prehistoric origins of Egyptian civilization, and are remnants of an ancient past dominated by animal husbandry, where the guardian of the flock, carrying a crook and flail, was the leader of the community.[26] In contrast, scorpion imagery associated with female deities seems to focus on the goddess's personal connection to the scorpions, and her intimate, often magical, knowledge of them. While Horus is often depicted physically dominating the animals, demonstrating his substantial power, the goddesses are able to harness the scorpion's power by using incantations, spells and by inspiring the animal's fierce loyalty. The different means of accessing the power of the scorpion by male and female figures in Egyptian royal and divine ideology suggests the complexity of cultural attitudes to gender. While female figures may connect emotionally with scorpions and use their intimate knowledge of the creatures to harness their power, for male figures the power of scorpions must be dominated or internalized physically rather than accessed through speech or magic. What unites the use of scorpion symbolism for both genders is the positive association with guarding: from female deities protection is often (but not exclusively) offered to children, pregnant mothers, family members and the king; while from male figures associated with kingship, protection is offered to the Egyptian kingdom and its people.

4 The Scorpion Weapon

My mind is full of scorpions.
Macbeth

The appreciation of the strength and ferocity of scorpions has led to their appearance in numerous historical conflicts. Scorpion imagery was a common decorative device on shields in ancient Greece, and swords with scorpion handles were thought to hold magical properties for the ancient warriors of Tibet. As well as having a defensive evocation, scorpions were utilized as an early form of biological warfare. The folklore of the scorpion that stings itself to death when surrounded by fire provided inspiration for abolitionists prior to the American Civil War.

Scorpions make dangerous adversaries. Their resistance to extremes of heat and cold, and ability to inflict mortal wounds on much larger opponents, as well as being naturally armed and shielded, mean that it is unsurprising that these diminutive arthropods have been adopted as allies in some of history's most well-known battles. The distinctive image of the scorpion, with its powerful pincers and raised stinger, makes an intimidating decorative element on shields and weapons, and its use in this capacity demonstrates the danger and warrior-like toughness that have historically been associated with this animal. Carrying an emblem of the scorpion promotes an image of aggression and efficiency. The Nigerian Army leader Brigadier Benjamin Adekunle (1936–2014) was given his nickname 'the Black Scorpion' for his involvement in the deaths of thousands of Igbo people, which

Fig. 1.

Fig. 2.

Fig. 3.

Fig. 5.

Fig. 4.

earned him the additional nickname 'the bloodhound of Nigeria'. The dominance of bellicose, violent behaviours associated with scorpion imagery seems to clash awkwardly with the reality of the animal's natural conduct. Most scorpions are not aggressive in a general sense, instead using their stings defensively when threatened.[1]

There are only a handful of reliable reports of the use of live scorpions against an enemy in conflict. This type of biological warfare seems to have been extremely effective – each historical mention of the deployment of scorpions in battle is accompanied by reports of victory, or of the psychologically damaging effect of the animals on enemy morale. Why then should the use of live scorpions in battle be so rarely reported? It seems likely

'Scorpio italicus', from August Johann Rösel von Rosenhof's 18th-century *Insecten-Belustigung*.

that the reason for the scarcity of this effective tactic may be the difficulties inherent in assembling these particular combatants safely. It has been noted that scorpions, being nocturnal in nature and frequently inhabiting desolate and dangerous terrains, are tricky animals to catch. This is the case for scientific researchers, and would also be true for anyone attempting to corral sufficient numbers of scorpions to be effectively deployed in battle. Like many powerful armaments of war, scorpions are an indiscriminate weapon. They are also renowned escape artists. The military strategist assembling large numbers of scorpions to release against an enemy may quickly find him- or herself facing 'blowback' in the form of an infestation of the fugitive arthropods. Despite these difficulties, scorpions have been successfully used as weapons of war.

Scorpion bombs were used in a conflict involving Roman besiegers in the Second Parthian War of 198–9 CE. Septimius Severus, the emperor of Rome, aimed to capture the desert fortress of Hatra, a city of tactical importance, which was full of riches gathered from the control of caravan routes. His troops had successfully taken the Parthian capital of Ctesiphon and conquered the northern half of Mesopotamia. Hatra was known to be wealthy, but also had a reputation as an impenetrable stronghold, after having repelled the siege of the Roman Emperor Trajan in 116–17 CE almost a century earlier. Faced with another Roman siege the inhabitants of Hatra, under the leadership of King Barsamia, filled clay-pot bombs with poisonous insects and sealed them up to hurl down upon their attackers.[2] Herodian, a historian from Antioch who reported on the siege, did not specify exactly what type of insects were involved, broadly describing them as 'poisonous flying insects'. In research detailed in *Greek Fire, Poison Arrows and Scorpion Bombs*, Adrienne Mayor makes a compelling case that the most likely inhabitants of the earthenware bombs were an assortment of scorpions, assassin bugs, wasps and other venomous insects from the area. Herodian describes the insects attacking the Romans' eyes and exposed skin, biting and stinging and causing severe injuries. Mayor suggests that the psychological terror caused by the downpour of diminutive adversaries may have been a decisive element in the Romans' choice to cut short their siege of Hatra after only twenty days, when similar sieges had lasted months or even years.[3]

The use of scorpions as biological weapons was recommended by the Byzantine Emperor Leo VI the Wise in his military treatise *Tactics*, in which he recommended hurling baskets full of scorpions and serpents on the enemy. The capacity for psychological damage caused by an arsenal of live scorpions was successfully exploited by the Viet Cong in the Vietnam War. The use of scorpions by the Viet Cong proved that a large quantity of the arthropods was not necessary to cause terror with entomological weaponry. During the war, large areas of Vietnam were peppered with a subterranean network of connecting tunnels. These spaces could be used as hiding spots by the Viet Cong, but also functioned as armouries, kitchens, first aid posts, dormitories and classrooms. When American soldiers unknowingly built a camp on top of these tunnels at Cu Chi, they realized that to gain control over the region above ground they would also need to defeat their enemies underground. An Australian field engineer unit, 3 Field Troop, were the first to successfully navigate the tunnels. Armed with pistols and knives, they were known as 'tunnel rats'. Searching the tunnels was extremely hazardous, as they were frequently booby-trapped with explosives or punji stake pits. Thin trip wires in the tunnels would instigate a deluge of venomous scorpions from hidden cavities in the roof, creating an atmosphere of horror.[4]

The terror of being in close confines with venomous scorpions was also exploited in Tibet. In the Tibetan town of Chusul there

is a cavern on the side of a mountain where legend says Tibetans who were condemned to death were walled in until the scorpions native to the area had served as their natural executioners.[5] While it is difficult to be certain of the historical accuracy of this story, the area is known to be densely inhabited by scorpions to the present day. A legend involving a scorpion prison is also told in the Mexican city of Durango. Durango has a long association with scorpions, one that continues to the present day – as can be seen in the name and symbolism of the city's football club, Los

Alacranes (the Scorpions). There were an average of 45 deaths per year due to scorpion envenomation in Durango in the years between 1890 and 1926. This astonishingly high rate of scorpionism ranked Durango as fourteenth in Mexico for scorpion fatalities in the period of study, with the highest rates of deaths from scorpion stings recorded in Colima and Nayarit, and southern Mexican states like Guerrero and Morelos. A local story has it that in 1884 a man named Juan was unjustly imprisoned in Durango. He was locked inside the 'death cell' from where no one had ever emerged alive after a single night's incarceration, due to the monster scorpion which inhabited the cell with the prisoners. Juan was able to capture the killer scorpion of the death cell, which resulted in his being pardoned and set free.[6]

In 2011 scorpions were allegedly employed as a weapon by a real estate company in the city of Shenzhen in southern China, in a dispute over property. Several thousand scorpions were released into a residential area, which was planned to be the site of a new construction project. The apartments in the complex had been scheduled to be demolished, but the residents had yet to complete deals for compensation. One of the residents told local news that he awakened to find a scorpion crawling across his body. Turning on the light, he was met with the sight of a room full of venomous scorpions.[7] The resident from the infested Chinese apartment complex managed with the aid of his family to capture several hundred scorpions in his home, and soon found the intrepid arthropods had been discovered in all of the apartments on the street. With the help of police, residents were able to catch over 50 kg (110 lb) of scorpions in a night. A witness reported seeing a man with a bucket leaving a real estate agency and then pouring something from the bucket into apartment windows. The real estate agency denied all involvement in the arachnids' release, saying that such a tactic would be too despicable to be employed, and would affect them also, saying: 'We wouldn't lift a stone only to have our own toes squashed.'[8]

Scorpions can be viewed as an effective tool to drive unwanted residents from their homes. As well as the real potential danger of the scorpions, there is also the emotional damage caused by the scorpions' aggressive reputation. Further, infestations of the arthropods are notoriously difficult to clear. Scorpions are capable of squeezing into tiny cracks and crevices to evade capture, and can withstand many sprayed insecticides. Even professional exterminators may struggle to remove the unwanted inhabitants. Exterminators usually work during daylight hours, while scorpions are active at night. Unlike an infestation of other bugs, such as ants, scorpions eat live food, so their food source can't easily be poisoned. Even if one were to succeed in applying a poison to the scorpion, their extreme hardiness may make this ineffective. One American exterminator explained the virtual indestructibility of the scorpion to the *Phoenix New Times*, recounting how he had captured a scorpion and placed it into a cup filled with the powerful pesticide chlordane. This particular pesticide was so toxic that its usage was banned in 2001. However, when the exterminator emptied the cup into the backyard after half an hour, the scorpion 'sauntered off into the desert'.[9]

The fear humans experience when faced with scorpions was utilized effectively in the ancient world, too. The symbolic usage of scorpions decorating shields, armour and weaponry can historically be traced back to ancient Greece, where soldiers adorned their shields with pictures of scorpions to frighten their enemies.[10] Spartan warriors utilized imagery from the temple of Artemis Orthia, the mistress of animals, as shield emblems, and these included scorpions. The feared Roman Praetorian Guard used the scorpion as their mascot. These elite troops formed the personal

bodyguard of the Roman emperors, and their association with scorpions may have originated with Emperor Tiberius, who had Scorpio as his zodiac sign.[11] A hexagonal shield carrying a scorpion blazon demarks a Praetorian Guard in the Great Trajanic Frieze.[12]

Recognition of the intimidation value of scorpion imagery has continued to the present day – the American professional wrestler Steve Borden, Sr, has used diverse scorpion symbolism to project an imposing image in a career spanning over three decades. Known by the ring name 'Sting', Borden was able to defeat fellow wrestler Hulk Hogan in a legendary match-up in 1997. Borden's success in the match was at least partially credited to the use of one of his signature moves, the Scorpion Deathlock (other signature moves include the Scorpion Death Drop and the Stinger Splash). Like the Spartans 2,000 years earlier, some of Borden's battle attire is decorated with images of the threatening-looking arthropods.

The scorpion is, in many cultures and stories, associated with magic rituals or witchcraft, which may either be protective

In this 18th-century etching by Ferdinand Landerer after M. Schmidt, a witch places a scorpion into a pot to make a potion.

or destructive. Images of scorpions have associations with spiritual battles as well as physical ones in Tibetan history. Scorpion imagery is thought to have adorned magical horns used by sorcerers in destructive rituals of black magic and exorcism. In rituals of destructive or protective magic, the depiction of a scorpion was connected to the subjugation of spirits.[13] A scorpion-hilted sword was wielded by several protective Tibetan deities. Lhamo, a principal deity charged with protecting the Tibetan government and the Dalai Lama, is a wrathful female deity who carries specific weaponry – a skull cup, a lance, a ritual sceptre and the scorpion sword. In Tibetan history, a warrior wielding a scorpion sword had access to special powers, being immune to the venom of the scorpion, and being able to control live scorpions for attacking the enemy.[14] The scorpion-hilted sword featured the black body and tail of a scorpion, with its sting forming the pommel (the enlarged top of the handle), the pincers the hilt and the flame-enveloped blade appearing as a long iron tongue from the creature's mouth.[15] It has been suggested that the sword probably had the capacity of stinging any unqualified person who might attempt to wield it. In Tibetan medical and religious traditions, the scorpion is perceived as having curative and coercive powers.[16] The guru Padmasambhava (known as the Second Buddha) was said to have received the *phurba* or 'ritual dagger' from a giant scorpion with nine heads and eighteen pincers.[17] The enormous scorpion unearthed the *phurba* from beneath a stone in a cemetery. The scorpion and its treasure led Padmasambhava to receive insights relating to spiritual accomplishment.

The name 'scorpion' has been popular among weapons at different times in history. In Europe, the 'scorpion' was a type of halberd with a deep and narrow blade. In India, it was another name for a type of knife, while in Egypt it was a type of short flail with weighted lashes. Perhaps most famously, the scorpion was

Silver Roman coin showing a scorpion beneath the horses' hooves.

a piece of Roman artillery. The scorpion catapult was greatly feared by enemies of Rome, and was famously used under the command of Julius Caesar in the Siege of Avaricum in the winter of 52 BCE. During the Siege of Amida in 359 BCE, rocks fired from a scorpion catapult were reported as causing massive casualties.

The dangerous and intractable power of scorpions was evoked by the man known as 'the father of the atomic bomb' to articulate the unprecedented risks presented by global nuclear war. J. Robert Oppenheimer, who led the Manhattan Project, lobbied for the regulation and control of nuclear power and strenuously opposed the arms race. Oppenheimer's exquisite awareness of the terrible destructive force of nuclear weapons is perhaps most poetically expressed in his famous quote taken from the *Bhagavad Gita*, 'Now I am become Death, the destroyer of worlds.' Oppenheimer also told the then U.S. President Harry S. Truman, 'Mr President, I have blood on my hands.'[18] Faced with a lack of nuclear reform, in July 1953 Oppenheimer wrote an article for *Foreign Affairs* called 'Atomic Weapons and American Policy'. In the article, he made the valid argument that the stockpiling of large quantities of arms could provide no security when the weapons involved contained such unprecedented destructive power. He likened the 'Great Powers' of the Cold War to two scorpions in a bottle, an analogy thought to have its origins in a Mexican blood sport:

An 18th-century ceremonial scorpion dagger, Eastern Tibet.

The Tibetan deity Lhamo, in *Shri (Palden Lhamo)*, central Tibet, c. 1750–1850, mineral pigments and gold on cloth.

The very least we can say is that, looking ten years ahead, it is likely to be small comfort that the Soviet Union is four years behind us, and small comfort that they are only about half as big as we are. The very least we can conclude is that our twenty-thousandth bomb, useful as it may be in filling the vast munitions pipelines of a great war, will not in any deep strategic sense offset their two-thousandth . . . The trouble then is just this: during this period the atomic clock ticks faster and faster. We may anticipate a state of affairs in which two Great Powers will each be in a position to put an end to the civilization and life of the other, though not without risking its own. We may be likened to two scorpions in a bottle, each capable of killing the other, but only at the risk of his own life.[19]

Oppenheimer's analogy has remained in the public consciousness up to the present day. It has been used to describe many conflicts in various parts of the world, from the battles between Greek and Turkish Cypriots in the 1960s to the conflict in the Middle East of the twenty-first century.

The natural strength and toughness of scorpions has led to the adoption of their imagery by military combatants for the purpose of intimidating enemies. In the struggle for the abolition of slavery prior to the American Civil War, scorpion imagery was used in a unique way that inverted this common usage. Instead of adopting the aggressive characteristics of scorpions as emblematic of themselves, the anti-slavery leaders used the idea of the scorpion which stings itself to death to illustrate their plan to defeat their adversaries. The earliest mention of this type of symbolism, as observed by James Oakes, Distinguished Professor of History and Graduate School Humanities Professor at the Graduate Center of the City University of New York, was in an English abolitionist journal that was republished by American abolitionists in the mid-1840s.[20] In January 1847 the board of the Massachusetts Anti-Slavery Society stressed the importance of the increasing public sentiment against slavery by using scorpion imagery, saying that when 'an enlightened public opinion' no longer tolerates pro-slavery sentiments, then:

The circle of fire which has already been kindled around the scorpion will grow hotter and hotter . . . until it will be compelled to bury its sting in its own brain, and rid the world . . . of its monstrous existence.[21]

By the 1850s this imagery of a self-destructing scorpion was no longer limited to the confines of New England abolitionism, with its usage becoming popular among anti-slavery politicians throughout the North.[22] The aptness of this analogy has been explained by Oakes, in his book *The Scorpion's Sting: Antislavery and the Coming of the Civil War*. The image of the scorpion driven to suicide perfectly captured the way that abolitionists expected slavery to die. Oakes notes that while the federal government was constitutionally unable to enter southern states and directly abolish slavery, what remained possible was to create conditions under which slave states would be pressurized to abolish slavery on their own.[23] The slave states would be surrounded by a 'cordon of freedom', cutting them off from federal support and denying them access to western lands, thus weakening them. As Oakes explains,

It was a perfect metaphor. Of course, it would not have worked if they knew the truth, that scorpions surrounded by fire don't really sting themselves, they go into convulsions that make it look as though they were committing suicide.[24]

We have noted that the power of the scorpion is usually either viewed as destructive or protective, but the usage of scorpion imagery by abolitionists is unusually complex – while the scorpion is seen as destructive, it is capable of bringing its own destructiveness to an end. It is also more common to adopt the destructive power of the scorpion (as many ancient kings did), rather than apply it to one's enemies. This rare subtlety can be viewed as a product of the delicate balance of political power prior to the war:

> It's the subtlety of the metaphor that made it so attractive to abolitionists. On one hand, it seems 'violent', yet in the end the violence is entirely self-inflicted. It helps to know that all of these people were haunted by the spectre of Haiti, where abolition was achieved by means of a bloody servile insurrection. Though the imagery seems violent to us, abolitionists thought of the 'scorpion's sting' as the peaceful alternative to the kind of brutal, protracted, military emancipation experienced in Haiti. Hence the paradox . . . of a seemingly violent act that was actually attractive because it was the alternative to war.[25]

Animal imagery in abolitionism is most often used to depict slaves, rather than the slave states; slave owners would dehumanize the slaves by associating them with, and treating them as, animals – debasing behaviour that was denounced by the abolitionists.[26] The nuanced and rare use of scorpion symbolism in the pre-war abolitionist movement gives insight into the language and ideas of a unique period of history.

In modern times, scorpions are a popular namesake for weapons of war, such as the Textron AirLand Scorpion, a tactical jet currently under development. As well as flying low-risk battlefield missions, the AirLand Scorpion is expected to be used to provide emergency relief for victims of natural disasters. The dynamic mobility of scorpions in the difficult terrain of a desert environment has led to research efforts to replicate this movement in the field of robotics. Wheels lack the flexibility of motion to traverse

difficult rocky ground, and so insects and other arthropods have become an important design platform to develop better adapted technology for use on pathways covered with rubble, commonly found in warzones, as well as debris found in the wake of natural disasters such as earthquakes and tsunamis.[27] Scorpions and other arthropods, such as crabs and lobsters, have been studied to attempt to advance the manoeuvrability of robots that may be used to find safe paths through minefields or to locate mines in clearing operations following conflict. The powerful venom of the scorpion has also been investigated for its use in military combat: the neurotoxin produced by scorpions has been studied for possible use as a biological weapon and scientists have even examined the possibility of modifying the scorpion's natural venom to make it more potent.[28]

The scorpion, in military terms, is a fully weaponized animal. While most dangerous creatures are polite enough to be hazardous only at one end, either end of the scorpion can inflict a killing blow to its foes.[29] Despite this, and the animal's intimidatingly thorough armament, the scorpion is not generally quick to seek out combat, preferring to conserve its stores of venom by escaping

Textron AirLand Scorpion at the 2014 Royal International Air Tattoo.

A scorpion, representing danger and protection, next to an armed warrior, adorns a sculpture at the Palazzo Ducale, Venice.

from danger courtesy of its many legs (an important exception to this trend is the pregnant scorpion, a creature best left entirely to her own devices). With a natural bounty of weaponry and an instinctive reluctance to deploy its most effective means of attack, there is some irony to the prevalence of scorpion imagery in historical human conflicts. In terms of the perception of the power of the scorpion as either dangerous or protective, both ideas can be seen to be a part of the historical association of scorpions with battle, while the choice of scorpion symbolism informs us about the values of combatants from a variety of historical periods and environments.

5 Scorpions in the Stars

Look for a scorpion under every stone.
Greek proverb

By the time that early humans had begun to look to the stars, and to tell stories about the great beings they observed among the constellations, scorpions had already inhabited the earth for hundreds of millions of years. Myths from a variety of ancient cultures identify the scorpion with Scorpius, a large constellation close to the centre of the Milky Way in the southern hemisphere. It contains the bright, supergiant star Antares, which is known for its distinctive reddish hue. The constellation is also home to several deep space objects, such as the star groups the Butterfly Cluster and the Ptolemy Cluster. The stars of Scorpius were recognized as depicting a scorpion in Babylonian times, and this association is also seen in the astrology of the Aztecs.

Four thousand years ago, the influential astrologers of Babylonia (the Chaldeans) observed the celestial movements of the sun, moon and the planets. Along with cultural developments in writing, these early Mesopotamian astronomer-scribes developed a foundational astronomy which showed sophisticated knowledge of the night sky. It has been suggested that these two momentous cultural events in Mesopotamia were closely linked: the development of writing led, in turn, to important advances in the investigative processes of early astronomy. The Mesopotamian astronomers recorded dates of heliacal risings – when a star becomes visible over the horizon before sunrise – and periods

Scorpius constellation.

when the planets were visible or invisible, along with detailed star lists and information on how various astronomical objects related to one another and to seasonal events. They grouped the most prominent stars from the night sky into twelve houses, one of these being Scorpio. These twelve houses were later given the title 'zodiac' by the ancient Greeks, who called them *zodiakos kyklos* or 'circle of animals'.

Religion and astrology were closely intertwined in the ancient world. Many Mesopotamian gods were closely associated with heavenly bodies; the Babylonian goddess of love and war, Ishtar, was associated with Venus, the morning and evening star. The

This hand-coloured map from 1856, the Burritt-Huntington Map of the Constellations, features an engraving of Scorpius, represented by a scorpion, in the lower right corner.

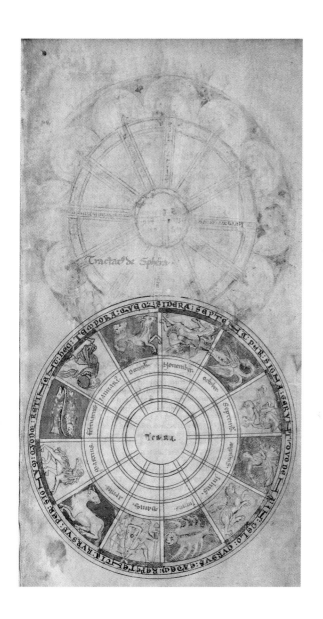

Late 12th-century
manuscript
diagram of
the zodiac.

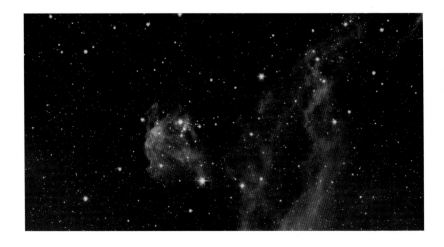

Babylonian word for Scorpius, *zuqaqipu*, means scorpion. The
movements and relative position of Scorpius were useful for the
work of Babylonian magicians and astrologers, who left written
records of the omens they observed, including cosmological traffic
updates: 'When a halo surrounds the Moon and Scorpio stands
in it, it will cause men to marry princesses, [or] lions will die, and
the traffic of the land will be hindered.'[1] A comet appearing in the
constellation was considered by astrologers to warn of a plague,
but when the sun rose in Scorpius, it was thought by alchemists
to be the only time when the transmutation of lead into gold
could occur.[2]

Although less common and less dangerous in Italy and
Greece than in the ancient Near East, scorpions still have a role
to play in Greek and Roman myth. It has been noted that the
appearance of scorpions in Greek and Roman myths may suggest
an oriental influence on the genesis of these stories.[3] The connection between astral bodies and religion is present in Greek
myths that concern the constellation. For the ancient Greeks,

Scorpius and Orion were closely linked. Scorpius was thought to be a giant scorpion, sent to earth by the primeval mother-goddess, Gaia. Accounts of the myths of Scorpius can be found in the works of several ancient authors, including Aratus and Ovid. The legend goes that the handsome giant and hunter Orion became confident that he was the most skilled of all in the pursuit of prey. He spent all of his time hunting, with Artemis

The constellation Orion from Johann Bayer's star atlas *Uranometria* (1603).

(the Greek goddess of the hunt) and Leto (Artemis' divine mother), and threatened to kill every creature on earth. This angered Gaia, who sent a giant scorpion to battle with Orion. The scorpion stung Orion, killing him. Artemis and Leto prayed to Zeus on their friend's behalf, and so Zeus placed Orion up in the stars. Zeus also placed the giant scorpion among the stars, as a memorial to him and the battle that had happened. On account of the conflict between them, the two combatants were placed

Simone Mosca (1523–1578), *The Fall of Phaethon*, marble relief.

as far apart from one another in the night sky as possible, to prevent them from ever coming together again. Despite this, it is thought that Orion has not forgotten the sting of his adversary, and flees across the night sky before Scorpius. As Scorpius ascends into the sky, Orion sets.

Scorpius is thought to have also frightened the Horses of the Sun while they were being driven by Phaethon, the young son of Helios (a Greek god thought to personify the sun). Phaethon lost control of the horses and nearly set the earth on fire, scorching the plains of Africa and creating a desert. Zeus was appalled by the boy's reckless destruction and killed him with a thunderbolt, causing his sisters, the Heliades, to mourn him.

Both of these Greek celestial myths involving Scorpius contain an intriguing ecological aspect. Scorpius battles to defend the earth's creatures from a voracious hunter in the first myth, and plays a role in the aetiological myth for the aridity of the desert. In Greek myth, the scorpion protects the natural world, but is also shown as intrinsically part of the natural world it protects. The frequent cultural association of scorpions and desert landscapes is expressed in terms of causality – the scorpion in Greek myth helped to shape the landscape of which it is an essential part.

Ancient Greek myths involving scorpions were not limited to describing celestial events. The famous King of Crete, Minos, is known in mythology for being the stepfather of the monstrous Minotaur. The Minotaur, who lived trapped in a labyrinth, was the offspring of Minos' wife, Pasiphae, and a great bull, which gave him his distinctive bull-headed appearance. Bestiality of various kinds seems to feature prominently in the marital relations of Minos and Pasiphae. Works ascribed to the second-century mythographers Pseudo-Apollodorus and Antoninus Liberalis describe the peculiar venereal disease of Minos:

Reliefs from Rome showing tauroctony, the icons of the ancient Roman cult of Mithras.

But if a woman slept with Minos, it was impossible for her to survive. Pasiphae had given Minos a drug because he slept with many women. And whenever he slept with another woman, he ejaculated poisonous creatures into her genitalia, and that is how they died.[4]

The particular species of 'wild creatures' ejaculated by Minos are snakes, scorpions and millipedes – all creatures known for their painful sting or bite – which would kill the women he had intercourse with.[5] This unusual sexually transmitted disease was given to Minos by Pasiphae in the form of a curse to attempt to stop her husband from being unfaithful. The myth provides the interesting (while eye-watering) angle of using snakes, scorpions and millipedes to, in a sense, personify the dangerous consequences of sexual infidelity.

Scorpions feature prominently in the iconography of the Roman cult of Mithras, popular in Rome around the second century when the Minos myths were also being written down. The cult of Mithras was thought to have been adopted by the Romans from Persian origins and the Persian deity, Mithras. Mithras-worship, or Mithraism, was discovered by findings depicting images of the god Mithras slaughtering a bull. The depictions were prominent in the cult's underground temples, or *Mithraea*, and in many of these scenes Mithras is accompanied in his bull-slaying activities by a dog, a snake and scorpion (sometimes also a lion). Textual evidence explaining the significance of these iconographic bull-slaying scenes is very rare, which makes a sure interpretation of the symbolism of the creatures involved extremely difficult. The scorpion is depicted grabbing the testicles of the bull, while the dog and serpent can be seen to lick the bull's blood. It is possible that the scorpion's placement may reflect its identification in Persian religious imagery, or possibly suggest its attachment to the bull's life-giving blood.[6] The scorpion's interest in the testicles of the bull, rather than its blood, may perhaps be due to the cultural link between scorpions and sexuality, seen in many ancient and modern cultures.

Thousands of years before the Greeks and Romans, and in a geographically distant location, the Australian Aboriginal people

Scorpion motif on the Friedberg krater, a pottery vessel from the Mithraeum, a Mithraic temple in Italy.

were also conceptualizing the stars of the constellation Orion with notions of hunting, and the stars of Scorpio as depicting a cosmic scorpion. Unlike Greek cosmological tradition, with its focus on the stars, Aboriginal astronomy focuses on the Milky Way and incorporates the dark patches between the stars.[7] For the Yolngu people of East Arnhem Land, the scorpion in the stars was named Bundungu, and was thought to be busily gathering his people along the banks of the Milky Way, which is traditionally called Milnguya. While the indigenous stories are not identical to the Greek myths, the identification of the constellation with a scorpion in both sets of myths seems remarkable, considering the differences in the two cultures, locations and historical settings.

A 2nd-century CE relief in Vienna showing the god Mithras slaying a bull, while a scorpion grasps the animal's genitals.

The burrowing scorpion, *Opistophthalmus carinatus*.

The celestial scorpion was also known to the people of ancient Mesoamerica. Both the Aztecs of central Mexico and the Lowland Maya are known to have had scorpion constellations. It is thought that these constellations may match up with the scorpion of the zodiac, but there is, as yet, no clear proof.[8] Among the Mayan people, the scorpion and its astral associations are called *Sinan* (meaning 'scorpion'). A depiction of this constellation is found in the Paris Codex, where a scorpion is portrayed hanging from a 'skyband', stinging an Eclipse of the Sun symbol.[9] It appears likely that the Maya viewed the celestial scorpion as an eclipse-causing agent.

THE ASTROLOGICAL SIGN OF SCORPIO

The scorpion is linked with the Western astrological sign of Scorpio, the eighth sign in the zodiac, and is the star sign attributed to people born between 23 October and 21 November. The ruling planets of Scorpios are Mars and Pluto, and its element is water. Famous Scorpios include Pablo Picasso, Hillary Clinton, John Cleese, Evelyn Waugh, Sam Shepard, Grace Kelly, Julia Roberts, Whoopi Goldberg, Winona Ryder, Bill Gates, Daniel Boone, Theodore Roosevelt, Mikhail Kalashnikov, Marie Curie and John Adams. The system of belief we now call astrology originated from the highest philosophical motivations and was viewed as a powerful force in the intellectual life of ancient Greece and Rome. Although condemned to near extinction with the rise of Christianity, astrology found a resurgence in the Middle Ages and once again permeated philosophy, literature and art.[10]

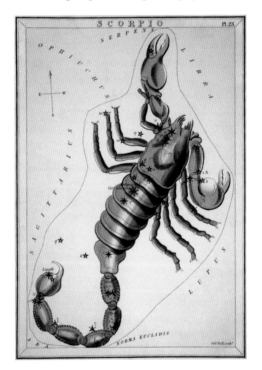

The Scorpio card from *Urania's Mirror*, a set of constellation cards first published in 1824.

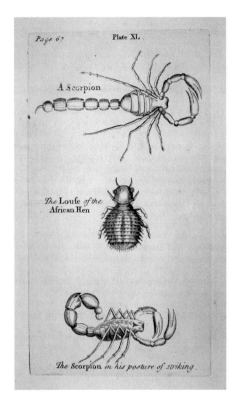

The powerful scorpion in its striking pose, by Eleazar Albin, in *A Natural History of Spiders and other Curious Insects* (1736).

Scorpio governs transformation; death and rebirth are its domain. Scorpios are known to go beyond the surface, accepting nothing in life at face value. Those born under the sign of Scorpio are considered passionate and intense, favouring the extremes in all forms. Positive aspects associated with the sign are the qualities of regeneration, transformation, healing, musicality, eroticism, magnetism, research, power and depth. More negative Scorpio qualities are destruction, violence, obsession, extremism, jealousy, vindictiveness, cruelty, suspicion and repression. Scorpio

Seventeenth-century fresco featuring figures of the zodiac, from the Svetitskhoveli Cathedral, 'The Living Pillar Cathedral', in Mtskheta, Georgia. Svetitskhoveli is known as the burial place of Christ's mantle.

is a water sign, and in astrology water is viewed as governing emotions. Although there are limits to sun sign astrology (that is, only accounting for where the sun, not the planets, fall in an individual's natal chart), there is generally harmony between signs of the same element. In this case, Cancer and Pisces typically find ease and flow with Scorpio. Earth signs are also commonly best suited to appreciate Scorpio's intense emotionality; Capricorn, Virgo and Taurus will commonly appreciate what the Scorpio has to offer. Taurus is Scorpio's opposing sign, and this 180° placement can be very potent. In astrology opposition is not necessarily a bad thing; the term 'opposites attract' comes from astrology for this very reason.[11] Very broadly speaking, the signs least harmonious to Scorpio are the signs that form a square (at a 90° angle); Aquarius and Leo both form a square to Scorpio (and Taurus on the opposite side), and thus these are often viewed as least compatible. Romantically, Capricorn, Cancer, Pisces and Virgo are generally best suited to Scorpio, if considered in line with the limits of sun sign astrology.

While fire signs – Aries, Leo and Sagittarius – claim to be the signs with the greatest sexual prowess, Scorpios too have a repu- tation as one of the most sexually attractive signs of the zodiac. According to the California-based astrologer and screenwriter Ryan Seaman, Scorpios are sexually distinctive, and the distinc- tion is energetic. Scorpios bring plenty of physical passion to their sexual activities, but are driven by uncovering what's underneath the surface of passion. They are thought to love the extreme nature of sex, and the raw emotional intensity it brings with it. Unlike those with fire signs, who are commonly out to satisfy their own pleasure, the Scorpio can fix his or her intense passion completely on the other.[12] Seaman explains how the symbolism of the scorpion relates to the personal qualities of Scorpios:

> Scorpios are known to sting, especially when they feel backed into a corner. Just as a Scorpion will sting itself to death, so too Scorpios may default to self-inflicted pain more readily than most other signs.[13]

THE SCORPION IN YOGA

We have seen that individuals with the Scorpio star sign are inter- ested in unearthing the subtleties of life, as well as getting beneath the surface of appearances. The practice of yoga can also be viewed as useful for getting beneath the superficialities of life and connecting with a deeper sense of meaning. The postures of yoga can assist in the exploration of the physical limits of the body, but on another level they also invite contemplation of mental and emotional bounds.[14] Yoga postures or *asanas* can be thought of as tools for awareness, and by 'sitting with' a particular pose, the essence of that pose can permeate the rest of the yogi's day, and even provide a sense of liberation.[15]

Yoga is one of the six orthodox systems of Indian philosophy, and the word *yoga* is a Sanskrit word meaning 'yoking' or 'connectedness'.[16] The *asanas* of yoga are often named after an ancient yogic sage, a sacred animal or legendary hero, and the myths or symbolism associated with the poses allow the physical aspects of the posture to have a deeper, more meditative side.[17] 'Scorpion pose' or *Vrschikasana* is an advanced yoga pose which involves an inverted backbend while balancing in a forearm-stand or handstand. The legs curl over the back like the tail of a scorpion. The posture develops stamina and endurance, strengthens the arms and the core muscles, and helps to increase the flexibility of the spine. The pose requires strength and great balance, and is only recommended for extremely advanced students of yoga. Ashley Turner is an acclaimed yoga and meditation instructor, author and psychotherapist who is based in California. According to Turner, Scorpion is one of the most challenging of all yoga poses, 'in a lot of ways', and comparable in difficulty to poses with a deep backbend or other arm balances such as *Eka Pada Koundinyasana* (twisted one-legged arm balance).[18]

Despite the ferocious image of the scorpion, the Scorpion pose is related to the inner search for harmony. With the pose's inversion of normal human stance, the yogi is essentially stamping on his head with his feet, and aiming to eradicate the self-destructive emotions and passions such as anger, jealousy and intolerance. The subjugation of ego then leads to harmony and happiness.[19] Ashley Turner explains the meaning of the posture: 'Scorpion pose asks us to move beyond ego, to find our tenacity and to open to possibilities we think might not exist.'[20] The difficulty of Scorpion may prove prohibitive for most practitioners of yoga (your author included), but there are other poses which, if safely accessible, can be used to build up towards the pose. The Scorpion pose requires strength and balance for the handstand, as well as great flexibility for the backbend.[21] Scorpion pose is one of the strongest yoga poses and, like the Scorpio star sign, one of the most magnetic and charismatic.[22]

Ryan Seaman performing a 'scorpion' yoga pose.

In yoga we find once again the human practice of symbolically adopting the natural power of the scorpion – as we have seen in the propaganda of ancient kings – but this power is harnessed in a unique way that is in keeping with the harmonious philosophy of yoga. Much like the practised yogi, the scorpion's imagery proves flexible yet powerful as it is adopted and shaped by varying cultural practices.

6 Scorpions on Screen and Beyond

> Whoever might perfume a scorpion will not thereby
> escape its sting.
> Hazrat Bahaudin Naqshband

Animal imagery has, from the most ancient times, been an integral part of human artistic expression. The scorpion's wide geographic range, ancient origins and dominance in human thought make it a common character in works of film, television, art and literature. Due to the popularity of scorpions in artistic media, the topic is sufficiently large to preclude its treatment here from being considered comprehensive. Instead, key examples will be given to expand on some frequent themes in the ancient arachnid's creative representation.

SCORPIONS ON SCREEN

Scorpions are frequently cast in the villain's role on the silver screen. It is difficult to think of an appearance of a scorpion in a film or television series where the animal was presented in a positive light (the *Scorpion King* franchise is arguably an exception). The forbidding portrayals of scorpions on screen most likely have their genesis in more ancient depictions of scorpions, which we have already examined here. The association of scorpions with wild and desolate natural environments, where the creatures seem to embody the inherent perils of these habitats, is evident in the Hebrew Bible, and this link continues in modern film. As well as presenting as a natural terror, scorpions in film show a distinct

connection to supervillainy – kind of an arachnid version of the cat-stroking villain archetype favoured in several films of the James Bond series. The appearance of scorpions on screen is not limited to these tropes. A more nuanced portrayal of scorpions is becoming more common, due to the popularity of the fable of the Scorpion and the Frog. We will consider the influence of the fable in this chapter, but will first consider depictions of dangerous deserts and arthropod-loving villains.

Animality is a central theme of the James Bond books and films. James Bond himself, with his insatiable appetite for sex and violence, is presented frequently in animal terms. In the novel version of *You Only Live Twice*, the villainous Blofeld is warned to be cautious in his dealings with 007, as 'this animal is danger-ous'.[1] Ian Fleming's Bond series is heavily fixated on 'the law of the jungle', where the forces of natural selection are constantly at play, meaning that the stronger characters survive while the weaker ones get eaten (often literally).[2] The focus on competitive struggle in Fleming's work sees political conflicts expressed in terms of predator and prey, and we see the scorpion included in this savage environment. Scorpions appear as part of the action in three Bond films: *Diamonds are Forever* (1971), *Die Another Day* (2002) and *Skyfall* (2012). In each of these films, scorpions threaten human life. A scorpion that is dropped down the shirt of a South African dentist is used as one of the unusual methods of assassination by Bond villains Wint and Kidd in *Diamonds are Forever*, and scorpions appear as one of several means of torture for 007 in *Die Another Day*. In the latter film, black scorpions crawl along the floor of Bond's cell, the scorpion's stinger receives a lingering close-up and a female torturer dangles a scorpion before Bond's face; the intercutting of scorpions as natural torture devices with the traditional silhouetted Bond girls in the film's title sequence lends an erotic tension to the opening credits, which has been criticized by some viewers for sexualizing torture.[3] Finally, a scorpion is featured perching precariously on Bond's hand in *Skyfall* as he takes part in a drinking game at an ocean-side bar. As Bond tilts

The Australian rainforest scorpion, *Liocheles waigiensis*. Unlike the stinging species used to torture James Bond, this species rarely stings, instead preferring to use its powerful claws.

his hand to drink, the scorpion raises its stinger, preparing to strike. Bond is able to drink sufficiently steadily to keep the scorpion from stinging, before capturing it in his empty, overturned glass. The scorpion scene informs the audience of Bond's character: he is a risk-taker, but evades the dangerous consequences of his risk-seeking behaviour through his stoicism. The scorpion's character, too, is expressed in the way it is shown in this scene not to sting without provocation. Although many scorpion stings undoubtedly occur without the creature first being harassed by a crowd of intoxicated bar-goers, the energy-depleting process of resupplying the sting with venom means it is in the scorpion's interest not to attack lightly.

The mixing of secret agents, evil geniuses and scorpions continues in the teen spy movie *If Looks Could Kill* (1991). *If Looks Could Kill*, a spoof of the James Bond formula, centres its plot on teen

Scorpions appear in drinking establishments in a number of ways, such as bottled spirits infused with scorpions.

agent Michael Corben (played by Richard Grieco) who must match his wits against the malevolent Augustus Steranko (Roger Rees). This supervillain is a megalomaniac, intent on creating an economically allied Europe, with one partner having a monopoly on all the wealth resources of the involved countries. Along with the film's intriguing depiction of global fiscal politics just prior to the founding of the European Union in 1993, it also features scorpions as the personal emblem of the evil genius Steranko. The personal assassin of Steranko, the evocatively named Areola Canasta (Carole Davis), uses live scorpions to kill her enemies. Similarly to the usage of scorpions in *Die Another Day*, the animals are portrayed in a manner which suggests they are both dangerous and erotic. Canasta attempts to seduce the young spy, and unleashes an extremely large scorpion onto his mostly naked body. This sequence ends with the assassin being 'hoisted by her own petard', when her pet scorpion falls inside her dress and inflicts a sting. The audience is left uncertain as to whether the sting would have proved fatal, as its victim is blown up shortly afterwards by another of Steranko's colleagues. The apparently orgasmic reaction of Canasta to the wound from the scorpion increases the scene's sexual innuendo. The combination of sex, danger and scorpions is also utilized in the political satire *War Inc* (2008), where Yonica Babyyeah (played by Hilary Duff) releases a scorpion into her pants, before asking a companion to reach into her trousers to remove it. The setting of this sequence in a bar would suggest that nightclubs are becoming a popular new habitat for scorpions.

The connection of sex, scorpions and supervillains can also be seen in the cult horror film *Dr Phibes Rises Again* (1972), the sequel to the classic film *The Abominable Dr Phibes* (1971). In the sequel, Dr Phibes (played by the legendary Vincent Price) arises from his sarcophagus in search of eternal life. He employs

Egyptian-themed methods for killing the assistants of his adversary, Darius Biederbeck (Robert Quarry). Using his beautiful assistant Vulnavia (Valli Kemp) as bait, Phibes lures one of his nemesis's unfortunate assistants to a scorpion-shaped throne, where the victim is trapped in the throne by sharp spikes. In his efforts to break free, he inadvertently releases the live scorpions that will sting him to death. The assistant screams while the scorpions crawl over him; Dr Phibes and Vulnavia listen serenely in the next room. The image of a live scorpion travelling inside the assistant's trousers creates a subversive contrast with his sexually suggestive pursuit of Vulnavia earlier in the scene. The pairing of scorpions and sexuality found in mainstream film culture is not new; we have seen scorpions symbolizing sexual energy in ancient Mesopotamia, where they were sometimes depicted in 'bed scenes' in Mesopotamian art.[4] More recently, in the popular culture of Indo-Pakistan, the arthropod is used to symbolize pain, lust and physical love itself.[5] The sting of the scorpion in this context represents the erect male sexual organ. Additionally, the scorpion is used on Moroccan women's textiles as a symbol of fertility, and to protect against sexual betrayal by a mate.

Continuing to explore the link in popular culture between villains and scorpions, we turn to a spoof of the James Bond series in *The Simpsons* episode 'You Only Move Twice' from its eighth season, which features a personable supervillain named Hank Scorpio. The cheerful evil genius (voiced by Albert Brooks) chooses Homer Simpson to come and work at his Globex Corporation. Scorpio's plans for world domination appear to include bribing the United Nations for gold, and torturing a spy named 'Mr Bont'. A song dedicated to Scorpio featured in the closing titles of the episode is a clear homage to the eponymous song from *Goldfinger* (1964), and its lyrics warn others to beware of the 'sting' of Scorpio, and his dreams of power and wealth. Another famous film antagonist associated with scorpions is Peter Pan's arch-nemesis, Captain Hook, in the movie sequel to the classic book by J. M. Barrie. Captain Hook (played by Dustin Hoffman) uses scorpions as punishment for errant behaviour from his pirate crew. The audience is led to believe Hook is about to discover a disguised Peter Pan (played by Robin Williams), but instead an unfortunate sailor (Glenn Close) is placed into a large trunk, called the 'Boo Box', and tortured with live scorpions.

The human conception of scorpions as predominantly dangerous, along with their recognition as powerful animals, has resulted in the frequent marriage of the scuttling arachnids with grandiose villains in cinema. A more realistic representation of the scorpion on screen can be found in the biographical war drama *Jarhead* (2005). In this film, American soldiers stationed in the Persian Gulf during the Iraq War entertain themselves by watching the blood sport of two scorpions fighting one another. The practice of gambling on the outcome of scorpions in battle either with each other or with different creatures has been recorded in several recent conflicts, including the Vietnam War.[6]

The use of scorpions to figuratively embody the dangerous power of nature can be seen in the classic horror film *The Black Scorpion* (1957), as well as *Transformers* (2007), *Indiana Jones and the Kingdom of the Crystal Skull* (2008) and *The Lone Ranger* (2013). Continuing a trope with a history stretching back to biblical times, in these films the menace of desolate, desert wildernesses is expressed by the film-makers through their use of scorpion symbolism. *The Black Scorpion* is a Mexican American horror classic, with impressive special effects by the pioneering stop-motion animator Willis O'Brien. The film begins with two devastating natural disasters, an earthquake and a volcanic eruption. From deep inside the newly formed volcano arise giant prehistoric scorpions, which go on a spree of destruction, killing local people

L

A D TE LEVAVI OCVLOS MEOS:
QVI HABITAS IN CÆLIS·ECCE SI
CVT OCVLI SERVORVM·IN MA
NIBVS DOMINORVM SVORVM
SICVT OCVLI ANCILLÆ IN MA
NIBVS DOMINÆ SVÆ ET CÆT.

Harrison Ford as Indiana Jones in *Indiana Jones and the Kingdom of the Crystal Skull* (2008).

and animals and destroying property. Through the help of a heroic entomologist, the primeval scorpions are eventually destroyed.

The use of action and horror in the films of the *Indiana Jones* franchise can be considered a signature element of the series.[7] In each film, our hero encounters swarms of fear-inducing animals. In *Raiders of the Lost Ark* (1981), Indy (played by Harrison Ford) is sealed inside a tomb with hundreds of snakes, which would be a problem for most people but is in this case especially challenging due to Indy's ophidiophobia (fear of snakes). The film's opening sequence also features large numbers of tarantulas inhabiting a booby-trapped temple in Peru. Indy has to deal with a tunnel of assorted insects beneath Pankot Palace in the sequel *Indiana Jones and the Temple of Doom* (1984). In *Indiana Jones and the Last Crusade* (1989), hordes of rats inhabit catacombs surrounding the tomb of a First Crusade knight beneath a Venetian library. *Indiana Jones and the Kingdom of the Crystal Skull* (2008) sees several of Indy's enemies fall prey to raiding army ants. Entering a Peruvian temple once again – seemingly undeterred from such endeavours by the past attacks of swarms of animals – Indy and his companion, Henry

Joris Hoefnagel and Georg Bocskay, *Rocket Larkspurs, Tulip, Scorpion, Millepede, and European Filbert*, 1561–2, watercolours and ink on parchment.

149

'Mutt' Williams (Shia LaBeouf), discover that it is inhabited by scorpions. Mutt is stung by one of the temple-dwelling arthropods as several scorpions scuttle free from inside a mummified body. Concerned about the possibly dire consequences of the venomous creature's sting, Mutt informs Indy of his injury, and asks if he will die. Indy asks after the size of the offending scorpion, and reassures Mutt that a bigger scorpion is less likely to harm him than a small one, adding: 'A small one bites you, don't keep it to yourself.'

The accuracy of Indy's assessment of the size to toxicity ratio of scorpions is reasonably good. Generally, it's not the larger scorpions with heavy pincers that are medically most concerning, but the smaller species with diminutively sized pedipalps which must rely on their more potent venom.[8] While a smaller scorpion may indeed be more likely to possess a more toxic venom, the size of the scorpion is an unreliable guide for the scale of the pain of the sting. The impracticality of judging the sting of a scorpion by its size was noted by the British entomologist William Sharp Macleay in a correspondence dated 3 January 1827. Writing of the benefits and detriments of his new home in Australia, he said:

> I was stung by an immense scorpion soon after my arrival, but was agreeably surprised to find the pain considerably less than the sting of a wasp, and of incomparably shorter duration. We must not judge of the pain of stings by the size of the insect which inflicts them.[9]

The appearance of scorpions in *Kingdom of the Crystal Skull* is also notable for the focus on the scorpions as a means for displaying Indy's experience and wealth of knowledge compared to his youthful companion. This is a common feature of the use of animals in the *Indiana Jones* film series, and the trope often contains a moral element. Natural hazards, such as army ants, falling boulders or ravenous crocodiles, perform as environmental obstacles that must be overcome by the intrepid archaeologist, demonstrating his superior survival skills and intellect, where frequently his less morally sound adversaries are carried away by ants, crushed or eaten. In the natural world inhabited by Indiana Jones, knowledge is a survival tool to be used when confronting the perils of the wild. This idea of the protective capacity of wisdom can be seen as a common theme in many myths and legends from the ancient world.

Scorpions are a threat to the Lone Ranger (Armie Hammer) and Tonto (Johnny Depp) in *The Lone Ranger* (2013), an action-packed Western based on the radio series of the same name. In one scene in the film, the Lone Ranger and Tonto are buried up to their necks in the desert, and menaced by scorpions. This scene illustrates how the natural danger of the desert wilderness is intensified in film by the addition of scorpions. The scorpions on set were managed by handlers, who were able to put the live scorpions in their mouths – a fact that contrasts the menace of the scorpions on screen with the less dangerous reality of the scorpions in real life. The risky feat of carrying live scorpions in one's mouth was also undertaken without known incident on the *Lone Ranger* set by the film's lead actor, Johnny Depp.[10]

Like the cult classic *The Black Scorpion*, Michael Bay's block-buster film *Transformers* (2007), based on the toy franchise from the multinational firm Hasbro, features a gigantic scorpion-creature. The film provides a vivid exploration of the theme of human relations with their technological advancements – especially in the fields of robotics and automation. This analysis takes the unusual narrative form of a battle of rampaging giant robots which transform into vehicles. In this context, animal characters provide a contrasting 'other' by which to judge the risks inherent in human technological advancement. The battle between Captain William Lennox (Josh Duhamel) and his force of Special Operations soldiers against the scorpion-shaped Decepticon, Scorponok, begins in a desert wasteland, heightening the sense of comparison between natural and man-made hazards.

Many other species of 'threatening' animals in the cinematic context are frequently depicted with exaggerated size: for example, car-sized spiders in the comedy horror movie *Eight-legged Freaks* (2002); giant snakes in the films of the *Anaconda* franchise (1997, 2004, 2008 and 2009); genetically engineered enlarged sharks in *Deep Blue Sea* (1999) and even super-sized ticks in the horror film *Infested* (1993). Although films featuring scorpions as a menace often show larger species of scorpion, in comparison to smaller ones which may be more toxic, there is a general trend against upsizing the scorpion dramatically. There are exceptions to this rule, such as *Transformers* (which features a kind of scorpion-machine) and *The Black Scorpion* (involving prehistoric scorpions). A further exception may be the scorpion adversary of *Honey, I Shrunk the Kids* (1989). In this case, the scorpion is no bigger than usual; instead, the film's shrunken protagonists are so diminished in size that they require rescue from the villainous arthropod by their new pet, the heroic, self-sacrificing baby ant 'Anty'. The general reluctance of film-makers to greatly exaggerate the size of scorpions in their films is likely due to the scorpions providing sufficient scares for the audience when portrayed at their natural size – in some ways, its small natural size adds to its menacing reputation, as the danger from its sting could easily go unnoticed.

A more nuanced role for the scorpion can be seen in an Oscar-winning film, Neil Jordan's *The Crying Game* (1992), where the fable of the Scorpion and the Frog is used to illustrate the main theme of the film – the inescapable influence of human nature on a person's actions. The use of the fable of the Scorpion and the

Frog in *The Crying Game* is the first in a series of recent usages for this story in the narratives of a diverse number of works of popular culture, including episodes of the television series *How I Met Your Mother* and *Teen Wolf*. The renaissance of the fable's popularity is likely due to the timelessness of its message. In the fable of the Scorpion and the Frog, described in the Introduction, Scorpion is, common to much of the scorpion symbolism looked at in this chapter so far, presented as dangerous, both to himself and to others. What is compelling and unique about the portrayal of the scorpion in this story is the lack of any moral element to the danger presented by the scorpion. The scorpion is hazardous, but this is simply due to his nature; he can't deny acting according to his natural instincts, even when it is clearly not in his best interest. Scorpion is not depicted stinging Frog because he is of bad character. Instead, Scorpion stings Frog because he is a scorpion, and it is in his nature to sting. The theme of the acceptance of the natural behaviour of the scorpion in this fable is an important one. Humans also have natural behaviours and instincts which, to an extent, circumscribe our actions and choices. Like the scorpion, the dominance of our animal instincts can at times outweigh what is perhaps in our best interest. The story of the Scorpion and the Frog is a powerful reminder of the inescapable and ever-present influence of our nature on our thoughts and actions.

In *The Crying Game,* the story of the Scorpion and the Frog is told twice, once in the first twenty minutes of the film, and again in the film's final scene, creating an overarching structure which bookends the events of the narrative. While a different character tells the story each time that the fable is told, both narrators are prisoners. This creates an intertextual link between the two tellings, and between the two narrators. At the start of the film, IRA (Irish Republican Army) soldier Fergus (played by Stephen Rea) kidnaps the British soldier Jody (Forest Whitaker). While guarding Jody and awaiting the fulfilment of the ransom demands, Fergus begins to form a bond of friendship with his prisoner, who tells him the story of the Scorpion and the Frog. In the supplementary material of the film's DVD release, writer and director Neil Jordan reveals that his inspiration to use the fable came from the classic Orson Welles film *Mr Arkadin* (1955), which features the use of the fable as a prelude to a toast in support of character. The use of the fable in the early scenes of *The Crying Game* reveals how characters on both sides of the conflict are shaped yet not defined by the larger political events which impact upon their natures. While Fergus is in a similar position to the other IRA members responsible for the kidnapping, Jody identifies his nature as kind, and this kindness is reflected in his humane treatment of his prisoner. In the closing scene of the film, Fergus is now the prisoner, incarcerated for the murder of a former IRA colleague. Fergus has become deeply romantically involved with Jody's girlfriend, Dil (played by Jaye Davidson, who, along with Stephen Rea, received an Oscar nomination for this film). When Dil visits him in prison, Fergus tells her the story of the Scorpion and the Frog. Fergus's kind nature and love for Dil, despite the differences between them, has led to his imprisonment, but also to a kind of redemption for the guilt he feels over Jody's death.

The fable of the Scorpion and the Frog has featured in episodes of several television series, including *How I Met Your Mother* ('The Scorpion and the Toad', Season 2, Episode 2), *Teen Wolf* ('Visionary', Season 3, Episode 8) and *Star Trek* ('Scorpion', Episodes 26 and 1, Seasons 3 and 4 respectively). The use of the fable in *Teen Wolf* features a dual narration, similar to what is seen in *The Crying Game*, although in this case the use of the story does not illustrate the similarities between two characters, but rather the unreliability of narration. The use of the fable of the Scorpion and the Frog is crucial to the characterization of the lead character of the crime thriller *Drive* (2011). The film's hero, who is an unnamed stunt driver (Ryan Gosling), is defined by the large yellow scorpion embroidered on to the back of his jacket. The director of the film, Nicolas Winding Refn, has said his use of scorpion imagery was inspired by the Kenneth Anger short film *Scorpio Rising* (1963). The use of the Scorpion and the Frog fable to explain the inherently violent character of the film's lead was suggested by the actor portraying the role, Ryan Gosling.[11]

SCORPIONS IN ART

The representation of scorpions began in art before appearing in literature. From the cave paintings seen in an earlier chapter, scorpions have inspired a wide range of creative responses, showing great cultural diversification. Even in the wide field of art, it is possible to observe the traditional dualism in human responses to the dynamic power of scorpions, with some portrayals focusing on the scorpion's destructive power, and some showing it in a protective role. The Spanish artist and sculptor Pablo Picasso was

Scorpion made of yarn, 1970s, Jalisco, Mexico.

thought to have said: '*Le cygne sur le lac fait le scorpion à sa manière*' (The swan on the lake is, in his own way, a scorpion).[12] This artistic metaphor expresses the idea of how symmetrically inverting the drawing of a swan's distinctively curved neck could be interpreted by the viewer as the curled tail of a scorpion with its stinger at the ready. The flexibility of scorpion imagery, being associated with dangerous or protective roles, can be seen by contrasting the symbolism of scorpions in Christian and Islamic art.

The scorpion, with its sting in the tail, is a symbol of treachery in Christian art, and therefore became a symbol of Judas. With its associations of betrayal, the scorpion is depicted on the shields and flags held by soldiers assisting at the Crucifixion of Christ.[13] The meeting of Christ with a scorpion is thoughtfully depicted by the British Neo-primitive painter Stanley Spencer, in one of his paintings from the series *Christ in the Wilderness*. In the painting *Christ in the Wilderness: The Scorpion* (1939), Christ is depicted sitting in the wilderness, tenderly cradling a scorpion, with its stinger raised, in the palm of his hands. The exposed palms of Christ and the position of the stinger creates an association with the Crucifixion. The slow curves of Christ's shoulders, juxtaposed against the rolling hills in the background, gives the impression of Christ as being at one with nature, and it is said that Spencer was impressed by Christ's empathy for such a dangerous animal as the scorpion, and the contrasting power of love.[14] Biblical imagery involving scorpions is also featured in literature, such as John Milton's *Paradise Lost* (1667), where their punitive emphasis is poetically alluded to: 'Back to thy punishment, /False fugitive, and to thy speed add wings, /Lest with a whip of Scorpions I pursue'.[15]

Attic bowl showing hunting scene with scorpions *c.* 680 BCE. The lid features dogs and nets used in the hunt.

In contrast to the malevolent portrayal of the scorpion in Christian art, we see the scorpion playing an apotropaic role in Islamic art and folklore. The scorpion, in the mystical imagery of Islam, can be seen as a symbol for the dervish's power of gaining mastery over evil.[16] There is a view that all creatures, even the most dangerous and venomous, are obedient to God and so become peaceful and tame in the presence of saints. Within Sufism, dervishes are instilled with magical powers enabling them to safely handle live scorpions. A similar divine protection from the sting of scorpions is thought to have been afforded to the enraptured. *Majzub*, a type of Muslim ecstatic, has the reputation of being able to touch any wild thing without being harmed. This is not to say that the scorpion in Islamic culture entirely lacks the menacing reputation seen, for example, in Christianity. Magic formulas and verses of the Quran have been used to gain protection from the sting of a scorpion, and have been inscribed on amulets and rings.[17] In Islamic art and crafts, scorpions can have a positive symbolism suggesting triumph over evil, or a hazard requiring divine protection. What is common to this symbolism is the superior power of God over dangerous animals.

The Italian Neoclassical sculptor Lorenzo Bartolini created his famous marble figure *Nymph with a Scorpion* (1845) in a classical style of artists from the early Renaissance.[18] While the sculpture is currently on display at the State Hermitage Museum in St Petersburg, the sculptor was commissioned to create the work by Prince Charles de Beauvau, a veteran of the Napoleonic Wars, and it was originally displayed at the 1845 Paris Salon. The sculpture contains a blend of mythical and realistic elements, with the nymph suffering the painful sting of the scorpion, which is depicted lying between her legs. Through the cradling of her foot and slightly perturbed expression on the face of the beautiful young nymph, Bartolini evokes the sense of a recent sting. There is a natural sense of movement in the piece, given through the fluidity of the lines of the naked young woman. The nymph's inspection of her sting takes her glance away from the audience, and it is thought that this imbues the work with a sense of innocence that makes it unique compared to the reclining female nudes of the Renaissance, such as those in the paintings of Giorgione and Titian.[19] The simple beauty of the piece has drawn many admirers, including the French poet Charles Baudelaire.[20] The sculpture demonstrates how the menace of the scorpion can be attractively depicted and given a subtle sense of eroticism.

The realistic depiction of scorpions in art was greatly furthered by the early German naturalist Maria Sibylla Merian (1647–1717). The detailed works of botanical art created by Merian have led to her being considered one of the most significant early contributors to the field of entomology. In particular, Merian's careful observation and documentation of the metamorphosis of the butterfly greatly enhanced scientific knowledge of the process. The intrepid naturalist spent two years in the Republic of Suriname, where she recorded the violence of the natural world in watercolours featuring two snakes fighting, as well as frog-eating scorpions. The accomplishments of Merian were appreciated by the English theologian and naturalist Lansdown Guilding who in 1831 wrote that 'We can never sufficiently admire the zeal of this female votary of the sciences.' In more recent times, the scorpion has been a popular subject for street artists, with a giant scorpion battling a beetle adorning the walls of an alleyway in Melbourne. In the UK, the street artist Ziml created an intricate image of a giant orange scorpion in Bristol's Jubilee Place.[21]

Some of the world's most celebrated writers have used the cultural symbolism of scorpions to convey powerful ideas in their works, and even to critique the works of other writers. In *The Common Reader*, Virginia Woolf described the works of Tolstoy as containing a treacherous 'scorpion', which deters the reader from fully embracing Tolstoy's depictions of happiness: 'There is always at the centre of all the brilliant and flashing petals of the flower this scorpion.'[22] The English poet Lord Byron utilized the familiar image of the scorpion which stings itself to death in his oriental romance, *The Giaour*:

> The Mind, that broods o'er guilty woes,
> Is like the Scorpion girt by fire,
> In circle narrowing as it glows,
> The flames around their captive close,
> Till inly search'd by thousand throes,
> And maddening in her ire,
> One sad and sole relief she knows,
> The sting she nourish'd for her foes,
> Whose venom never yet was vain,
> Gives but one pang, and cures all pain,
> And darts into her desperate brain;
> So do the dark in soul expire,
> Or live like Scorpion girt by fire.[23]

In the footnotes accompanying the poem, Byron amusingly shows his doubts over the veracity of the myth of the suicidal scorpion:

Alluding to the dubious suicide of the scorpion, so placed for experiment by gentle philosophers. Some maintain that

Bartolini's *Nymph and the Scorpion*, 1845.

Scorpion graffiti.

the position of the sting, when turned towards the head, is
merely a convulsive movement; but others have actually
brought in the verdict '*Felo de se.*' The scorpions are surely
interested in a speedy decision of the question; as, if once
fairly established as insect Catos, they will probably be
allowed to live as long as they think proper, without being
martyred for the sake of an hypothesis.

It has been noted that the light-hearted footnote from the poet
serves to undermine the dramatic tension of the scorpion imagery
in the poem, placing fictional imagination within the realm of
scientific experiment.[24] This rapid switch of genre, from pathos
to parody, demonstrates the malleability of scorpion imagery in
literature as well as the impressive range of the poet.

Perhaps the most famous of recent written works involving
scorpions is *Night of the Scorpion*, by the Indian Jewish poet
Nissim Ezekiel (1924–2007). This poem uses the drama of the
injury from a scorpion as a narrative device to explore the fortitude

162

of the poet's mother, and her powerful love for her children –
showing an interplay with the ancient connection of scorpions
and protective mother figures. The poet describes the panic of
the family and their neighbours as his mother is tortured by the
venom of the scorpion for twenty hours. It describes the fruitless
attempts to locate the offending scorpion, and the folklore surrounding its sting. In the last three lines, once her suffering has
eased and the wound has 'lost its sting', the poet finally gives a
voice to the mother. Up until this point, the reader has observed
the poet's mother through the eyes of her child, allowing no
insight into her perception of her own situation. When her feelings about the night's events are revealed, they carry a powerful
emotional impact:

> My mother only said:
> Thank God the scorpion picked on me
> And spared my children.[25]

Another Indian-born writer, Rudyard Kipling, also wrote of
scorpions. Kipling's talent for writing animal characters is most
familiar to modern audiences from *The Jungle Book* (1894). In 1893
Kipling published the short story 'The Children of the Zodiac'.
While quite melancholy in tone, the narrative addresses the relations of mortals to gods, and how the fear of dying can imprison
the living. Kipling divided the zodiac signs into Children of the
Zodiac (the Ram, the Bull, Leo, the Twins and the Girl) and
the Six Houses (the Scorpion, the Balance, the Crab, the Fishes,
the Archer and the Waterman). The Six Houses prey upon the
Children of the Zodiac, with the Scorpion stinging and killing
the Bull. Although the Bull dies quickly from his wound, the fear
of the scorpion's sting had kept him furrowing the farmer's fields
for many years before it occurred. The main protagonist of the

story is Leo, who is killed in the end by Crab, but who teaches Kipling's overall lesson: 'that whatever comes or does not come we men must not be afraid'.

Animal imagery in the works of Shakespeare is frequently used to aid in characterization, 'to define the nature of man'.[26] The success of Shakespeare's usage of colourful animal symbols in his work can be seen in the continued popularity of some of his expressions in modern speech, such as 'the smallest worm will turn, being trodden on', from *Henry vi*, 'the cat will mew and the dog will have its day', from *Hamlet*, and 'making the beast with two backs' from *Othello*. In Shakespeare's powerful tragedy *Macbeth*, the eponymous Scottish general laments: 'Oh, full of scorpions is my mind, dear wife!' (iii.2). This striking

Nineteenth-century scorpion seal.

image allows the audience access to Macbeth's continual state of mental anguish, as he is repeatedly 'stung' by venomous thoughts. Scorpion imagery is used twice more in works of Shakespeare (in *Henry vi* and *Cymbeline*), and in all of these examples the focus of the symbolism is the sex–power relationships between an elite couple – Macbeth and Lady Macbeth, Queen Margaret and Henry vi, and Cornelius and Cymbeline.[27] The connection between scorpion imagery and treacherous or ambitious women is further seen in the thirteenth-century monastic manual *Ancrene Wisse*, where it is written that a man who grasps a woman is like one grasping a scorpion, and that a scorpion is similar to a woman with the tail of a serpent; it flatters with its head, but stings with its tail.

A more subtle allusion to gender politics, along with the use of scorpion imagery to depict feelings of desolation and wildness in the natural environment, can be found in Jack Kerouac's novel *Desolation Angels* (1965). In Chapter Fifteen the protagonist, Jack Dulouz, watches a baseball game at dusk, standing beneath a tree at a dirt-road crossing. He comments on the bleakness of the prevailing winds, before recalling his companion volunteering to show him a scorpion. Lifting a rock, the female scorpion is revealed alongside the skeleton of her mate, who she has cannibalized. Jack's companion crushes both scorpions with a rock, to Jack's approval. As a pedantic side note, it is unlikely either of the novel's characters could have known the gender of the two scorpions. Sexing scorpions is largely dependent on internal factors and provides a great deal of difficulty even for specialists. Also, cannibalism in scorpions is not restricted to the hazards of mating, with scorpions preying on one another opportunistically. Despite these details, the use by Kerouac of scorpions in *Desolation Angels* heightens the sense of alienation and bleakness in the protagonist's environment. The post-coital cannibalism also subtly

Yellow-banded flat rock scorpion, *Hadogenes trogloytes*, from South America.

raises the issue of violence and disconnect between the sexes in the text.

Scorpions, along with centipedes, were also featured in Sir Arthur Conan Doyle's second Sherlock Holmes novel, *The Sign of Four* (1890). The use of these creatures effectively gives the city of Agra a sense of desolation, and also foreignness:

> But the modern part is nothing like the size of the old quarter, where nobody goes, and which is given over to the scorpions and the centipedes. It is all full of great deserted halls, and winding passages, and long corridors twisting in and out, so that it is easy enough for folk to get lost in it. For this reason it was seldom that anyone went into it.

Pinturicchio, *St Jerome in the Wilderness*, c. 1475–80, oil on canvas.

The use of scorpions to suggest dangerously desolate natural environments in literature may suggest the influence of their evocation of this sense in the Bible. Additionally, the isolation of deserted places is in itself perceived as providing a suitable

atmosphere for dangerous crimes by the great detective in *The Adventures of Sherlock Holmes* (1892), where he explains to Dr Watson:

> The pressure of public opinion can do in the town what the law cannot accomplish. There is no lane so vile that the scream of a tortured child, or the thud of a drunkard's blow, does not beget sympathy and indignation among the neighbours, and then the whole machinery of justice is ever so close that a word of complaint can set it going . . . But look at these lonely houses, each in its own fields . . . Think of the deeds of hellish cruelty, the hidden wickedness which may go on, year in, year out, in such places . . . [28]

In the examples of scorpion symbolism from literary works considered in this chapter, there has been an emphasis on its dangerous sting, overshadowing all other aspects. However, the representation of the scorpion in literature can be used to more understated effect, without losing any of its dramatic impact. During the Second World War, many *Nisei* (second generation Japanese Americans) entered the armed services, with regiments such as the 442nd earning an unprecedented number of decorations for valour in combat. At the same time, their families were incarcerated in 'War Relocation Camps', spread across the USA and Canada. 'The Rattlesnake and the Scorpion' is a poem by Dr Ruth Yoshiko Okimoto, who was interned with her family at a camp in Poston, Arizona. The poem takes the form of a dialogue between a rattlesnake and a scorpion, who have been observing the construction of the Poston camp. The Rattlesnake and the Scorpion complain of the noise of the construction, and the loss of their hunting grounds and food source. The Scorpion tells the

Rattlesnake that members of his family are being captured by the builders and drowned in alcohol. The Scorpion wonders why humans would try to encroach on the animals' ancient claim to the land – their 'sacred place' – when humans only wish to 'ravage and destroy' while the animals remain peaceful, without ill intent.

The ancient origins of the scorpion, and its usurpation by the builders of the camp, are sensitively evoked by the author, drawing comparisons with the displacement of the land's traditional owners, the Native Americans. Poston Camp was built on the Colorado River Indian Reservation, and the free, forced labour of the *Nisei* was exploited by the u.s. government to build infrastructure on the site, so that following the war it could be used to consolidate the scattered Native American tribes from smaller, geographically distinct reservations into one place.[29] The Rattlesnake explains to the Scorpion that differences in skin colour or thought can be used as a pretext by some humans for 'justifiable hate'. The composition of the poem, three years prior to the bombing of Hiroshima, shows an almost prescient awareness of the danger of human-made weapons by the poet. The Rattlesnake gives the Scorpion this ominous warning:

'As you know,' continued the Rattlesnake,
'humans are the most dangerous animal of all;
they kill with lethal weapons ten feet tall.'[30]

SCORPIONS IN VIDEO GAMES

The last mention of scorpions in artistic media in this chapter must go to the rapidly expanding field of video games. When compared with film, art and literature, video games are quite a recent form of entertainment, having only developed in the last 50 years or so. The anatomy and image of the scorpion is used

in the blockbuster video game franchise *Mortal Kombat*, in the characterization of the player and sometime boss-figure of Scorpion. Despite his two-dimensional genesis, Scorpion is a fairly complex character. Originally a Japanese ninja, Scorpion is killed by his arch-nemesis, Sub-Zero. Scorpion and Sub-Zero have a legendary enmity, with Scorpion seeking vengeance in the form of a revenant (a kind of revitalized spectre) on his chilly rival. The freezing capacity of Sub-Zero is deliberately contrasted by the game's creators with the fiery, hot-blooded aspect of scorpion imagery, and creates an interesting clash of natural elements. Despite some scorpions living in freezing conditions, their predominance in desert environments has created an association with fieriness, which is ironic considering the popularity of the myth of the scorpion killing itself when

surrounded by fire. Perhaps this myth contains a moral about the benefits of moderation – 'nothing too much', as the wisdom of the ancient Greeks suggests. In any case, Scorpion is enhanced by his arthropod-like qualities, including his spear, which he is able to use in battle to draw an opponent close to inflict a devastating and often fatal attack, accompanied by his catchphrase, 'Get over here!' The use of animal and supernatural elements in the *Mortal Kombat* franchise adds to the epic feel of the game, while demonstrating the continued popularity and relevance of scorpion imagery in varied artistic media.

7 The Sting in the Tail

Great indeed is the power of the dragon as the sun,
Yet humbly and slowly it meanders its way shy,
Minuscule indeed is the power of the tiny scorpion,
Yet it swaggers its tail and boasts to the sky.
Old Thai verse

Scorpions and humans have lived alongside each other for tens of thousands of years, and have something of a tumultuous history with one another. While frequently admired or even revered for their protective strength, the fear of scorpions has led to an affixation on the sting in their tails, often at the expense of their many other remarkable qualities.

In recent years, scorpions have become increasingly popular as a subject for body art. While we tend to think of tattooing as a fairly recent phenomenon, the history of this practice extends all the way back to ancient Egypt. Mummified corpses from various cultures have been discovered bearing body art. Among the tattooed Egyptian mummies currently known, the best preserved is that of Amunet, a priestess of the goddess Hathor who lived during the Eleventh Dynasty (2160–1994 BCE).[1] The forms of her tattoos are dots, dashes and an elliptical symbol on her lower abdomen.

The tattooed remains of an Iron Age horseman was discovered in 1948 by the Russian archaeologist and anthropologist Sergei Ivanovich Rudenko. The body was of a Pazyryk chieftain, who seems to have been aged about 50 years old when he died, and who was very strongly built. The Pazyryk culture is closely linked to that of the Scythians, a nomadic Iranian equestrian tribe. The chieftain's many tattoos included pictures of animals, such as a donkey, a ram and two deer, alongside more fantastical creatures, such as griffins and monsters. He also bore a series of simpler circular tattoos along his spine. This remarkable find demonstrates the ancient origin of body art depicting animals, a trend that continues in the modern age.

While tattooing has been practised for thousands of years, the cultural significance of tattoos has changed greatly across history. In Greek and Roman times, tattoos were signs of ownership for slaves and also identified prisoners. Tattoos, in other contexts, could also signify a sense of belonging. Roman soldiers were sometimes marked with tattoos to show their membership of a specific legion. Charles Darwin noted the prevalence of tattooing among the indigenous tribes that he studied, which were often intended to display membership of a community.

The ornamental tattoos of modern popular culture can also be thought to express a sense of belonging, or a connection to

A desert hairy scorpion, *Hadrurus arizonensis*, on a rock in North America.

the artwork's subject. This is often the case for tattoos of insects and arachnids. An influential study published in 1989 found that the motivation of Americans to get tattoos generally fell into one of five categories: as a symbol of an interpersonal relationship; participation in a group; self-identity/magical protective significance; as a decorative/aesthetic statement; or a representation of key interests or activities. Tattooing has been described as art at its most intimate, while at the same time being appealingly accessible.[2]

Scorpion tattoo.

The tattooing of dangerous arthropods on one's body has been practised historically in a number of cultures as a kind of artistic 'insecticide'.[3] A nineteenth-century author commented on this function of body art in Indian culture, noting how in Jaipur people would carry the mark of the scorpion, and added that this practice in Malay culture showed the wearer's desire to express both fear of and respect for the creature.[4] In modern culture, the influence of astrology has made crabs and scorpions the most popular arthropod designs, and the great popularity of these tattoos is also thought to be due to the animal's reputation as nature's diminutive 'bad-ass'.[5] It is intriguing to note that the scorpion's toughness and celestial connections are frequent motivators for wearers of this kind of art – meaning that tattoos are one of the few representative artistic media where the focus on the danger of the scorpion's sting doesn't overshadow its more positive qualities. In his fascinating article, 'Insect Tattoos on Humans: A "Dermagraphic" Study', published in *American Entomologist*, G. A. Pearson notes that the rise in popularity of 'insect' tattoos signifies a more positive attitude towards arthropods in some sections of the public. He also discovered that most wearers of insect tattoos were women, a somewhat surprising find considering the stereotypical view of women as being the gender especially squeamish around bugs.

As well as adorning our bodies with their image, humans have begun to investigate the potential use of scorpions and their venom to provide new medical breakthroughs. The possible medicinal properties of scorpion venom are only now becoming known to scientists, and there are many questions that remain to be answered. It was reported in 2013 that a medical doctor vacationing in Mexico experienced a surprisingly beneficial side effect after having been stung by a bark scorpion. Following the administration of antivenin, the man found he had an overwhelming reduction in pain from a chronic autoimmune disease he had suffered from for eight years, ankylosing spondylitis (a type of spinal arthritis). Two years after the sting, the doctor remained largely free from pain and had been able to come off most of his medications. Although it may be premature to attempt to establish a direct causal relationship between the scorpion sting and the turnaround in the man's health, he was reported to have said that if the pain returned, he'd allow himself to be stung a second time![6]

Australian scientists from the University of Queensland recently published the results of their study into the neglected medical potential for many varieties of scorpion venom. The findings of the study presented 'tremendous implications' for therapeutic use.[7] The results of the study have particular significance for developing new types of pain relief, with the numbing effect of some scorpion stings showing promise for developing new analgesic medicines. The pain caused by some types of scorpion sting is also of scientific use, to better understand how pain is caused and therefore how to more effectively reduce it. The antimicrobial properties found in the venom of some species of scorpion have great potential to yield powerful new ranges of antibiotic medicines, used to treat infections. The overuse of antibiotics in agriculture, medicine and the food industry has led to an increase in multi-drug-resistant bacterial strains, one of the most important health issues in recent years.[8] Scientists have already successfully developed a new antibiotic, Vejovine, from the venom of the black scorpion *Vaejovis mexicanus*, which is frequently found inhabiting narrow spaces within Mexican households. The continued discovery and characterization of more proteins with antibacterial properties from other species of scorpion holds promise for the development of further new treatments for multi-drug-resistant bacteria.

The notorious efficiency of the venom of scorpions to kill their insect prey has led to research into possible new types of insecticides. In 1994 British scientists successfully tested the world's first genetically engineered pesticide, developed from the venom of a North African scorpion. The new pesticide was found to effectively kill certain species of caterpillar and moth. Research is continuing on developing new types of scorpion pesticides which could safely protect agricultural enterprise without the environmental hazards of traditional pesticides.

Emperor scorpion.

A molecular biologist working in the field from the University of Tel Aviv was quoted in a report from *ABC Science* as saying that scorpions could be considered 'a gift from nature'.[9] The venom of scorpions has developed over millions of years to effectively target the nervous systems of their prey; harnessing this capability may help in the safe production of food. The scorpion toxins have the advantage of being biodegradable, so they are unlikely to accumulate in ground or drinking water, as traditional chemical pesticides do. Overcoming resistance to commonly used chemicals in other creatures, such as mosquitoes, is also important in the global fight against malaria. The World Health Organization estimates that in 2012 there were over 200 million cases of malaria worldwide, resulting in over half a million deaths. The venom of scorpions has been enlisted to aid in the battle against insecticide-resistant mosquitoes which host the malaria parasite. Combining scorpion antimicrobials with a slow-acting fungus is thought to make an effective insecticide which is 'evolution-proof' and likely to greatly improve efforts to eradicate the disease.[10]

Scorpion venom has been used widely in the traditional medicines of China, Africa and India for thousands of years. One species showing particular potential for future medical breakthroughs is the Chinese golden scorpion *Mesobuthus martensii*, also known as the Manchurian scorpion. Its habitat is in China, Mongolia, Korea and Japan, and the species was discovered by Westerners in 1879, when the German arachnologist Ferdinand Karsch observed specimens in the grounds of the Peking Summer Palace. Traditionally in Chinese medicine, this type of scorpion has been used to treat problems such as epilepsy, chronic pain and paralysis; however, in recent years the unique components of the scorpion's venom have been shown to have anticonvulsant properties, as well as having analgesic and antitumour properties

A confined Australian scorpion.

which hold promise for improved future treatments against cancer. A 2014 study showed that many scorpion venoms are exhibiting potential for many different types of anticancer therapy.[11] In recent scientific trials, nanoparticles embedded with proteins from scorpion venom have been successfully used to kill cancer cells.[12] While scientists have been aware of the incredible capacity of scorpion venom to kill cancer cells, there is a critical stumbling block to this beneficial feature of scorpion venom: the difficulty in safely delivering the venom to cancer cells without harming the human body. By delivering the venom via nanoparticles, early trials suggest scientists may have overcome this obstacle, with the treatment thought to be available for human use in approximately five years, if animal trials continue to be successful. When embedded in the nanoparticles, the scorpion venom has been shown to have an even greater effectiveness at killing cancer cells

A pseudoscorpion (also known as a book or false scorpion).

than in its pure form, with an increase of nearly ten times its natural toxicity.

While not true scorpions, book scorpions are notable for their contributions to the conservation of literature. Book scorpions are pseudoscorpions, a close arachnid 'cousin' to the scorpions of this book. These tiny scorpion-like creatures (around 4 mm or 0.2 in. long) have played an often overlooked yet crucial role in preserving the world's ancient written texts. Book scorpions feed on booklice and dust mites. Left unchecked, these parasites would have chomped their way through many famous works of literature, but instead their populations are curtailed by the predatory vigilance of book scorpions.[13] It is not only the great written works of the ages which enjoy the protection of these scorpion-like guardians; recent research has suggested book scorpions may have a critical role to play in the conservation of bees. The massive global decline in the populations of bees, known as 'colony collapse disorder', poses a serious threat to global biodiversity. Bees are essential for the pollination of flowering crops, which are necessary for the provision of food. It is believed that a type of mite (the varroa or 'vampire' mite) is one of the leading causes of the dropping number of bee populations, which have seen a decline in size of between a quarter and a third in recent years in Europe and the United States collectively.[14] While chemicals can be used against the mites, there are concerns that the chemicals' toxicity may be detrimental to the health of the bees and the natural environment. In the 1950s book scorpions were documented as having a symbiotic relationship with bees; the pseudoscorpions hunt the mites, grasping them with their pincers and then eating them. In this way, the bees are cleaned of parasites and the book scorpions find a steady food source. The use of book scorpions has proved successful in reducing the numbers of varroa mites in bee populations within laboratory conditions, and researchers in Hamburg are investigating whether these small book-conserving creatures could play a larger role in global efforts to conserve bee populations.[15]

Much like the cryptic creatures themselves, the beneficial aspects of scorpions and their venoms are only in the early stages of being studied and understood. The scientific study of scorpions holds promise for a bright future for the relations between scorpions and humans, and one that could greatly benefit human health, agriculture and the environment. However, the destruction of scorpions' natural habitats, and their endangerment through being overharvested for the exotic pet trade, means several species of scorpion are currently threatened. Often, the hazards of deforestation, urbanization, pollution and eco-toxicity, along with mining and industrialization, mean that some species of scorpion may be vulnerable to extinction as they only occur in a geographically small area. For example, five species of scorpion from the Western Cape province of South Africa are listed as threatened, with a decrease in population of over 80 per cent projected in the next three generations.[16] Among these is the black-legged burrowing scorpion, *Opistophthalmus fuscipes*.

Scorpions are predatory creatures, creating a further complication in their conservation. As an 'apex predator', a decrease in the numbers of scorpions in an ecosystem has a destabilizing effect.[17] Scorpions help to maintain environmental balance, providing bio-controls for other insects such as aphids and flies. Removal of apex predators from an ecosystem has been shown to lead to population changes in the creatures that they would traditionally prey upon. An example of this 'top-down trophic cascade' is the disappearance of wolves from Yellowstone National Park, and the resulting increase in numbers of elk. The elk consumed such large volumes of young willow trees that they then began to starve, with the lack of willow trees also affecting the area's beaver population. In the case of scorpions, so little is known of these cryptic creatures that it is extremely hard to predict the environmental consequences of any diminishment in their biodiversity.

Although their toughness is legendary, scorpions themselves are surprisingly vulnerable to extinction, due to small litter sizes, long generation times and low survivorship for sexually immature females.[18] As some of the most understudied and poorly understood creatures on earth, many species of scorpion may become extinct before they can be discovered. Anecdotal evidence suggests that some species of scorpion may have already disappeared.[19] The dearth of knowledge on various types of scorpion and their life cycles and habitats means that even if we are aware of threats to the survival of a type of scorpion, more research would be needed to inform us about the best method of assisting that scorpion's survival. A great deal of scorpion conservation to date has been incidental, where efforts to preserve an ecosystem, or a charismatic animal within that ecosystem, have resulted in the happenstance protection of scorpions living within that ecosystem. This type of conservation is not ideal; not every species of animal responds well to the 'hands off' approach to conservation – there are many species which thrive on human contact and interaction.[20] Some varieties of scorpions may be among these 'urban adapters' who source food and shelter from human contact, but further research is needed to better understand which human endeavours are helpful or harmful for the survival of scorpions.

It is not only a lack of scorpions that is problematic. Habitat degradation can also lead to an explosion in the number of scorpions found in an area. Overgrazing in agriculture can create arid environments which are preferred by some species, and unfortunately it seems to be the scorpions that are dangerous to humans which seem to benefit in this way from a disturbed environment, leading to a corresponding increase in scorpionism. These more opportunistic scorpions then tend to prey on the other scorpions in the area, further disturbing the balance of the ecosystem and scorpion biodiversity.

As well as being useful as 'bio-indicators', whose disappearance can alert us to habitat degradation, it has been suggested that the enduring appeal of scorpions may make them useful 'flagship' species in the battle to preserve endangered habitats.[21] Threats to the natural environment of scorpions can certainly serve to remind us that if this ancient group of arachnids is struggling, we must take the issue of habitat degradation seriously, for the benefit of all creatures. However, the appeal of scorpions, while obvious to many, is perhaps not universally acknowledged – scorpions are not known for their cuddliness. The stigma of the scorpion, when viewed purely in terms of its potential for damaging humans, has historically created a sociological barrier for accessing the funding and research attention needed in the varied fields of study related to the scorpion. Even when the scorpion's appeal is recognized, this in turn can be a kind of double-edged sword for the animal's survival. One of the greatest threats to many well-known types of scorpion is overharvesting for the exotic pet trade.

The illegal trading of wildlife is creating a conservational catastrophe among many of the world's most vulnerable species. The trade is a multi-billion-dollar industry, which is often run by criminal syndicates, operating in remote regions and exploiting local people.[22] With the trade in illegal wildlife now worth at least $19 billion annually, it ranks among drug trafficking, arms smuggling and the trafficking of human slaves in terms of illicit profit.[23] Along with the trafficking of humans, animal trafficking has been identified as one of the largest growing illegal markets, and frequently the networks used by cartels for illegal wildlife trading are also utilized for other criminal trade, such as weapons or drugs.[24] The growth of the illegal wildlife trade in the past ten years has been significant. This increase has been fuelled by an upsurge in affluence in regions where animals are sought for their use in traditional medicines or, in the case of scorpions, their appeal as novelty pets.[25] The illegal nature of this business lends itself to secrecy, which in turn makes collecting estimates of the environmental cost of wildlife trading difficult. The enormous amounts of money at stake and the involvement of major criminal networks also makes attempts to stop wildlife trading inherently dangerous.[26] However, illegal wildlife trading can be viewed as on a par with deforestation for its ability to negatively impact on animal and plant species, leading to the extinction of many.[27] The danger to the global environment presented by wildlife trafficking is twofold, involving a loss of biodiversity and the transmission of zoonotic (transferred between species – animals to humans) and other diseases.[28]

In September 2014, Chinese quarantine officials working in Shantou, Guangdong province, intercepted around 100 scorpions in parcels sent from Germany.[29] Six kinds of scorpions were among the smuggled animals, including *Androctonus australis*. The large numbers of scorpions involved in this smuggling operation are not surprising, considering the scale of the trade internationally. While habitat degradation is currently the greatest threat to the survival of many types of scorpion, the exotic pet trade, especially coming out of Africa and parts of Latin America, is having a disastrous impact on scorpion numbers.[30] Southern California is a hub for the exotic pet trade. Recently, live scorpions bound in stuffed animals were intercepted by California's Department of Fish and Wildlife, who then enlisted a scorpion expert from the Natural History Museum of Los Angeles to help unwrap the hidden arthropods.

Emperor scorpion.

Pandinus imperator on sand.

Unlike capturing scorpions for scientific study, which is done in limited numbers and by researchers with knowledge of the impact of removing scorpions from an ecosystem, scorpion poaching involves sustained collecting of scorpions over a long period of time, and can result in the removal of thousands of animals. For example, in the years 1995–6, approximately 105,000 *Pandinus imperator* scorpions were exported from three small West African countries.[31] The popularity of an animal in the exotic pet trade has been causally linked in some species to its endangerment, as has been the case with the Mexican *Brachypelma* tarantula, which was so heavily traded that it was added to Appendix II of the CITES list (meaning that its trade must be strictly monitored).[32] The exotic pet trade is focused on profit rather than preservation, with the mark-up on the eventual sale of the animal sufficiently high that even 90 per cent mortality rates have been seen not to deter animal traffickers.[33] Recently, the harvesting of scorpions has flourished in Pakistan, risking irreparable loss of biodiversity and the likely increase in other species of animals that are not beneficial to the environment.[34] Though the market price for scorpions is extremely high (it is reported that 60 g, or just over 2 oz, black scorpion could be valued at more than $50,000 and in 2007 the *Wall Street Journal* reported scorpion venom to be worth $39 million per gallon in a comparison of liquid prices),[35] the individuals involved in the actual capture of the scorpions receive very little money and, it has been reported, risk being abducted themselves by cartels.[36] There are thought to be two markets for the unregulated but lucrative trade in scorpions: large pharmaceutical companies who wish to harvest their venom, and foreign workers in Pakistan who view scorpions as food.[37]

A food stall in Thailand selling fried insects and scorpions.

The presentation of a scorpion inside a lollipop reflects the tendency to market the creatures as a 'novelty' food item.

Seahorses and scorpions on skewers.

As well as being overharvested for the pet trade, scorpion numbers are being depleted internationally due to their popularity as food. Areas of Southeast Asia and China in particular have many species of scorpion on the menu, and the sale of scorpions for novelty food is a growing market for tourists. While some of the scorpions on offer are farmed for this purpose, others will have been taken from the wild.

SCORPIONS IN THE FUTURE

The study of scorpions is still in its very early days. Very little information is available about the behaviour, ecology and general biology of most species of scorpion that are currently known. As well as this, it has been recently acknowledged that there is a much greater diversity of scorpions than previously thought – while we have around 2,000 known species, it is likely that the actual number of species globally is around three times

189

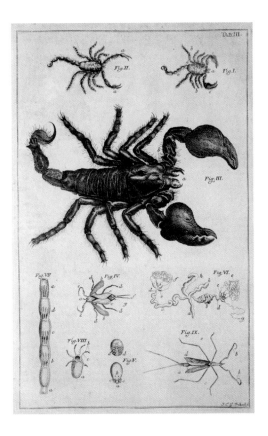

Giant scorpion from Jan Swammerdam, *The Book of Nature* (1737).

as high.[38] Increased funding and more research are required in all the myriad of fields related to scorpiology, such as medical and behavioural research, studies into biodiversity and taxonomic relationships, ecological studies, venom toxicology, scorpion anatomy and genomic analysis (such as gene sequencing) and adaptive physiology.

Scorpions have a lot of knowledge to impart to us, not only in terms of their own qualities but in regard to the world's ecosystems, both past and present. Scorpions are ancient creatures that are long-lived and slow-growing, which makes them attractive as a model system to gain insight into the evolution of life on earth. The study of scorpions can assist in understanding patterns of continental drift, past climate change and the great events of earth's history. As well as this, scorpions are innately fascinating, and it is worthwhile to continue attempting to gain a greater understanding of these mysterious creatures.

CONCLUSION

The scorpion, in many ways, is a misunderstood animal with a bad reputation that can at times overshadow its many exceptional qualities. As was wryly noted in a recent scientific article on the useful aspects of scorpion venom, 'Fables have long cast scorpions as bad-natured killers of hapless turtles that naively agree to ferry them across rivers.'[39] The story of the Scorpion and the Frog has surfaced numerous times in this book, and it serves as an important reminder of the dominance of our animal nature on our thoughts and actions. It is of crucial importance for us to understand and accept our natural limitations and boundaries. However, there is a variant of this story, thought to be a Buddhist proverb, which is worth considering. This version is called 'The Old Man and the Scorpion':

One morning, after he had finished his meditation, the old man opened his eyes and saw a scorpion floating helplessly in the water. As the scorpion was washed closer to the tree, the old man quickly stretched himself out on one of the long roots that branched out into the river and reached out to rescue the drowning creature. As soon as he touched it, the scorpion stung him. Instinctively the man withdrew his hand. A minute later, after he had regained his balance, he stretched himself out again on the roots to save the scorpion. This time the scorpion stung him so badly with its poisonous tail that his hand became swollen and bloody and his face contorted with pain. A young boy who observed this approached the old man and asked why he persisted in trying to help a creature which would only sting him for it. The old man replied: 'Just because it's the nature of the scorpion to sting, that doesn't change my nature, which is to save.' The old man thought about the problem, and then picked a leaf from a nearby tree. Using the leaf, he was able to pull the scorpion from the water and save its life, without being stung.[40]

This version of the story illustrates the idea that, while it's wise to be aware of our natural instincts and their influence on our behaviour, the careful application of wisdom and knowledge can help us to direct our instincts in a manner beneficial to ourselves and our environment. In doing so, we may also become successful 'super-adaptors', like our scorpion neighbours.

Timeline of the Scorpion

430 MYA	c. 3100 BCE	c. 3000 BCE	c. 2100 BCE
First known scorpions appear on land	Narmer Palette in ancient Egypt depicts a Predynastic king with a scorpion	Cave art in Tennessee depicts humans and scorpions	Sumerian poems detailing the epic adventures of Gilgamesh, featuring the mysterious gate-keepers, the Scorpion Men

2nd century CE	12th century	1551
Scorpion bombs used against Roman beseigers in the Second Parthian War	Modern English word 'scorpion' develops from Middle English, from the Old French word *scorpion*, which can be traced back to ancient Greek	Conrad Gessner's *Historiae animalium* published. Gessner makes the observation that scorpion mothers carry their young on their backs

1957	1960s	1990	1997
Mexican American cult horror film *The Black Scorpion* released by Warner Brothers	French scientists discover scorpions capable of surviving an atomic blast	Gary A. Polis produces the 'scorpion bible', *The Biology of Scorpions*, influencing a generation of scorpiologists	Professional wrestler Sting defeats Hulk Hogan by using his signature Scorpion Deathlock manoeuvre

1279 BCE	c. 721 BCE	c. 350 BCE

Drawing of rare double-tailed scorpion inscribed into the tomb of New Kingdom Pharaoh Seti I

Atalia, queen of the Assyrian Empire, decorates royal personal items with scorpion symbolism

Known scientific study of scorpions begins with Aristotle's *History of Animals*

900–1500 CE	1667	1860s

Depictions of a giant scorpion monster found in the Madrid Codex

John Milton's *Paradise Lost* poetically reinforces the punitive emphasis of allusions to scorpions in the Book of 1 Kings

First recording of the colony of yellow-tailed scorpions *Euscorpius flavicaudis* in the county of Kent in southeast England. Known locally as 'Sheerness scorpions', it is thought they sailed to England on Italian shipments of masonry

2002	2007	2015

The Scorpion King film, starring Dwayne 'The Rock' Johnson, is released, making a worldwide box office of over $150 million

Comparing the prices of liquids in response to a proposed boycott of gasoline, the *Wall Street Journal* reports scorpion venom is worth $39 million per gallon

New research shows that a genus of South American scorpions can drop their tails, as well as part of their gut, to escape from predators by providing a decoy

References

INTRODUCTION: SHINING A LIGHT ON SCORPIONS

1 Tertullian, *Scorpiace* 1.1.
2 J. P. Chippaux and M. Goyffon, 'Epidemiology of Scorpionism: A Global Appraisal', *Acta Tropica*, cvii/2 (2008), p. 77.

1 A BASIC GUIDE TO THE BIOLOGY OF SCORPIONS

1 Natalie Angier, 'The Scorpion, Bizarre and Nasty, Recruits New Admirers', www.nytimes.com, 27 November 1990.
2 J. A. Coddington and R. K. Colwell, 'Arachnida', in *Encyclopedia of Biodiversity*, ed. S. C. Levin (New York, 2001), pp. 199–218.
3 Ibid., p. 208.
4 W. R. Lourenço, 'Diversity and Endemism in Tropical versus Temperate Scorpion Communities', *Biogeographica*, lxx/3 (1994), pp. 155–60.
5 W. R. Lourenço and A. Pézier, 'Addition to the Scorpion Fauna of the Manaus Region (Brazil), with a Description of Two New Species of *Tityus* from the Canopy', *Amazoniana*, xvii (2002), pp. 177–86.
6 Wilson Lourenço, 'Scorpion Diversity in Tropical South America', in *Scorpion Biology and Research*, ed. Philip Brownell and Gary A. Polis (Oxford, 2001), p. 412.
7 Ibid.
8 Mohamed A. Abdel-Rahman, Patrick L. Harrison and Peter Strong, 'Snapshots of Scorpion Venomics', *Journal of Arid Environments*, cxii (Part B) (2015), pp. 170–76.

9   Mark A. Newton, *A Guide to Keeping Australian Scorpions in Captivity* (Adelaide, 2008), p. 18.

10 Thomas Eisner, *Secret Weapons: Defences of Insects, Spiders, Scorpions and other Many-legged Creatures* (Cambridge, MA, 2005), p. 6.

11 Roland Stockmann and Eric Ythier, *Scorpions of the World* (Verrières-le-Buisson, 2010), p. 7. It should be noted that scorpion experts believe the actual number of species is likely to be much higher.

12 Gary A. Polis, 'Ecology', in *The Biology of Scorpions*, ed. Gary A. Polis (Stanford, CA, 1990), p. 249.

13 Laurence Pringle, *Scorpion Man: Exploring the World of Scorpions* (New York, 1994), p. 13.

14 Ibid.

15 J. Pizarro-Araya, A. A. Ojanguren-Affilastro and L. Prendini, 'First Report of an Arboreal Scorpion (Bothriuridae: *Urophonius*) from the Temperate Forests of Southern Chile', *Gayana (Concepción)*, LXXV/2 (2011), pp. 187–91.

16 Pringle, *Scorpion Man*, p. 13.

17 Lorenzo Prendini, 'Scorpiones', www.accessscience.com, accessed October 2014.

18 Ibid.

19 Professor Lorenzo Prendini, personal communication, 19 September 2014.

20 Gary A. Polis and W. David Sissom, 'Life History', in *The Biology of Scorpions*, ed. Gary A. Polis (Stanford, CA, 1990), p. 163.

21 Ibid., p. 168.

22 Ibid.

23 Ibid., p. 169.

24 Rod Preston-Mafham and Ken Preston-Mafham, *The Encyclopaedia of Land Invertebrate Behaviour* (Cambridge, MA, 1993), p. 15.

25 Fred Punzo, *Desert Arthropods: Life History Variations* (New York, 2000), p. 82.

26 W. R. Lourenço, 'Parthenogenesis in Scorpions: Some History – New Data', *Journal of Venomous Animals and Toxins Including Tropical Diseases*, XIV/1 (2008), pp. 19–44.

27 Sarah Zielinski, 'Beware the Pregnant Scorpion', www.sciencenews.org, 3 June 2014.

28 Michael R. Warburg, 'Scorpion Reproductive Strategies, Potential and Longevity: An Ecomorphologist's Perspective', in *Scorpions 2001*, ed. Victor Fet and Paul A. Selden (Burnham Beeches, 2001), p. 349.

29 M. Vannini, A. Ugolini and I. Carmignani, 'Mother–Young Relationship in *Euscorpius:* Adaptive Value of the Larval Permanence on the Mother's Back (Scorpiones, Chactidae)', *Journal of Arachnology*, XIV (1986), pp. 43–6.

30 Vincent H. Resh and Ring T. Cardé, eds, *Encyclopedia of Insects* (New York, 2009), p. 908.

31 A. H. Rowe et al., 'Voltage-gated Sodium Channel in Grasshopper Mice Defends Against Bark Scorpion Toxin', *Science*, CCCXLII (2013), pp. 441–6.

32 Wayne Lynch, *Owls of the United States and Canada* (Baltimore, MD, 2007), p. 103.

33 J. David Ligon, 'The Biology of the Elf Owl, *Micrathene Whitneyi*', *Miscellaneous Publications Museum of Zoology, University of Michigan*, CXXXVI (1968), p. 37.

34 David Attenborough, *Life in the Undergrowth* (London, 2005), p. 23.

35 Mattoni C. I. et al., 'Scorpion Sheds "Tail" to Escape: Consequences and Implications of Autotomy in Scorpions (Buthidae: *Ananteris*)', *PLOS ONE*, X/1 (2015), e0116639.

36 Robert C. Anderson, *Scorpions: The Ancient Arachnids* (Pocatello, ID, 1983), p. 14.

37 Ibid.

38 Attenborough, *Life in the Undergrowth*, p. 23.

39 Zia Nisani, 'Behavioral and Physiological Ecology of Scorpion Venom Expenditure: Stinging, Spraying, and Venom Regeneration', PhD dissertation, Loma Linda University, 2008.

40 Eisner, *Secret Weapons*, p. 20.

41 Pringle, *Scorpion Man*, p. 9.

42 David Cheng et al., 'Scorpion Envenomation', http://emedicine. medscape.com, accessed 30 June 2014.

43 Eisner, *Secret Weapons*, p. 18.

44 Anderson, *Scorpions: The Ancient Arachnids*, p. 16.

45 Ibid.

46 Steve Backshall, *Venom: Poisonous Creatures in the Natural World* (London, 2007), p. 96.

47 'Not a Scratch: Scorpions May Have Lessons to Teach Aircraft Designers', www.economist.com, 4 February 2012.

48 Cheng, 'Scorpion Envenomation'.

49 Ibid.

50 Leslie M. Frost et al., 'A Coumarin as a Fluorescent Compound in Scorpion Cuticle', in *Scorpions 2001*, ed. Victor Fet and Paul A. Selden (Burnham Beeches, Bucks, 2001), p. 365.

51 Ibid.

52 C. T. Kloock, 'Aerial Insects Avoid Fluorescing Scorpions', *Euscorpius*, XXI (2005), pp. 1–7.

53 M.L.M. Lim, M. F. Land and D. Li, 'Sex-specific UV and Fluorescence Signals in Jumping Spiders', *Science*, CCCXV (2007), p. 481.

54 Douglas D. Gaffina et al., 'Scorpion Fluorescence and Reaction to Light', *Animal Behaviour*, LXXXIII/2 (2012), pp. 429–36.

55 '13 February 1960: The First French Nuclear Test', www.ctbto.org, accessed June 2014.

56 Max Goyffon and Vincent Roman, 'Radioresistance of Scorpions', in *Scorpion Biology and Research*, ed. Philip Brownell and Gary A. Polis (New York, 2001), p. 393.

57 Ibid., p. 403.

58 Stockmann and Ythier, *Scorpions of the World*, p. 155.

59 Brian Handwerk, 'Scorpions Thrive Where Least Expected', http://news.nationalgeographic.com.au, 24 June 2003.

60 Attenborough, *Life in the Undergrowth*, p. 23.

61 Stockman and Ythier, *Scorpions of the World*, p. 155.

62 Attenborough, *Life in the Undergrowth*, p. 23.

63 Richard J. Williams, Malcolm A. Gill and Ross A. Bradstock, eds, *Flammable Australia: Fire Regimes, Biodiversity and Ecosystems in a Changing World* (Collingwood, NJ, 2012), p. 205.

64 Jean-Henri Fabre quoted in Marco Colombo, 'On Fabre's Traces:

An Important Contributor to the Knowledge of *Buthus occitanus*
(Amoreux, 1789)', *Euscorpius*, CXVII (2011), p. 2.

65 Aristotle, *History of Animals*, Book IV.

66 David M. Williams and Malte C. Ebach, *Foundations of Systematics and Biogeography* (New York, 2008), p. 228.

67 Hisham K. El-Hennawy, 'Scorpions in Ancient Egypt', *Euscorpius*, CXIX (2011), p. 12.

68 Ibid.

69 Victor Fet and Paul A. Selden, 'On the Pioneering Contributions of Francesco Redi and Holder Jacobeus to the Anatomy and Reproductive Biology of *Euscorpius flavicaudis* (De Geer, 1778) in the Seventeenth Century (Scorpiones: Euscorpiidae)', in *Scorpions 2001: In Memoriam Gary A. Polis*, ed. Victor Fet and Paul A. Selden (Bucks, 2001), p. 383.

70 Ibid.

71 Alfred G. Bourne, 'The Reputed Suicide of Scorpions', *Proceedings of the Royal Society of London*, XLII (1887), pp. 17–22.

72 Colombo, 'On Fabre's Traces', p. 6.

73 Victor Fet, 'Obituary: Gary Allan Polis (1946–2000)', *British Arachnological Society Newsletter*, CXXXIX (2000), pp. 14–15.

74 Professor Lorenzo Prendini, personal communication, 19 September 2014.

2 SCORPIONS IN PREHISTORY AND THE ANCIENT WORLD

1 Dr Robert W. Gess, personal communication, 27 May 2014. This interview has been edited for publication, and any resulting inaccuracies due to reordering the material are the responsibility of the author.

2 Gondwana was the more southerly of two ancient supercontinents that existed between 510 and 180 million years ago. It was made up of the land masses now known as South America, Australia, Antarctica, Madagascar and India.

3 Dr Robert W. Gess, personal communication, 27 May 2014.

4 Ibid.

5 Jason A. Dunlop, O. Erik Tetlie and Lorenzo Prendini,
   'Reinterpretation of the Silurian Scorpion *Proscorpius osborni*
   (Whitfield): Integrating Data from Palaeozoic and Recent
   Scorpions', *Palaeontology*, CI/2 (2008), p. 312.
6 For a thorough overview of the scientific association of scorpions
   and eurypterids, see Jason A. Dunlop and Simon J. Brady,
   'Scorpions and their Sister-group Relationships', in *Scorpions
   2001: In Memoriam Gary A. Polis*, ed. Victor Fet and Paul A. Selden
   (Burnham Beeches, 2001), pp. 6–8.
7 Dr Robert W. Gess, personal communication, 27 May 2014.
8 Ibid.
9 Roland Stockmann and Eric Ythier, *Scorpions of the World*
   (Verrières-le-Buisson, 2010), p. 22.
10 S. Zhu et al., 'Experimental Conversion of a Defensin into a
   Neurotoxin: Implications for Origin of Toxic Function', *Molecular
   Biology and Evolution*, XXXI/1 (2014), pp. 546–59.
11 Joel N. Shurken, 'How the Scorpion Got its Venom', *Inside Science*,
   www.insidescience.org, accessed April 2014.
12 Jan F. Simek et al., 'Sacred Landscapes of the South-eastern USA:
   Prehistoric Rock and Cave Art in Tennessee', *Antiquity*, LXXXVII
   (2013), pp. 430–46.
13 Ibid., p. 443.
14 Andrew R. George, 'The Epic of Gilgamesh', in *The Cambirdge
   Companion to the Epic*, ed. Catherine Bates (Cambridge, 2010),
   pp. 1–12.
15 S. Dalley, trans., 'Enuma Elish, Tablet 1', in *Myths from
   Mesopotamia* (Oxford, 1989), p. 237.
16 Nadine Nys, 'Scorpion People: Deadly or Protective?', *Studia
   Mesopotamica*, I (2014), p. 59.
17 Ibid.
18 Gene Kritsky and Ron Cherry, *Insect Mythology* (San José, CA,
   2000), p. 94.
19 J. K. Rowling, *Harry Potter and the Prisoner of Azkaban* (London,
   1999), p. 164.
20 Gene Kritsky, 'The Insects and Other Arthropods of the Bible,

the New Revised Standard Version', *American Entomologist*, XLIII (1997), p. 183.

21 See, for example, ibid., p. 187; W. F. Browning, *A Dictionary of the Bible* (Oxford, 2009), p. 324; David Noel Freedman, ed., *Eerdmans Dictionary of the Bible* (Grand Rapids, MI, 2000), p. 1172; Herbert Lockyer Snr, ed., *Illustrated Dictionary of the Bible* (Nashville, TN, 1986), p. 62; Paul J. Achtemeier, *Harper's Bible Dictionary* (New York, 1985), p. 912; B. C. Birch, 'Scorpion', in *International Standard Bible Encyclopedia Q–Z*, ed. Geoffrey W. Bromiley [1915] (Grand Rapids, MI, 1988), pp. 357–8; and Burton L. Goddard, *Animals and Birds of the Bible* [1976] (2009), p. 31.

22 For the word as a type of weapon see, for example, J. L. Cloudsley-Thompson, 'Scorpions in Mythology, Folklore and History', in *The Biology of Scorpions* (Stanford, CA, 1990), p. 468; John A. Davies, *1 Kings* (Darlington, 2012), pp. 240–41; Lockyer Snr, ed., *Dictionary*, p. 62. For the sceptics of this view, see Anselm Hagedorn, *1 & 2 Kings: A Continental Commentary* (Minneapolis, MN, 2003), p. 143; John Jarick, *2 Chronicles* (Sheffield, 2007), pp. 90–91. Jarick suggests the Israelites may be 'bitten' by scorpions, which one imagines would be more pleasant than being stung by them, while still being generally undesirable.

23 For example, Ralph W. Klein, *2 Chronicles* (Minneapolis, MN, 2012), p. 160, who does provide the reader with a few good options for interpretation while keeping above the fray.

24 For more on the interpretation of scorpions as a 'harmful' gift that would not be given by a loving father see, for example, Joel B. Green, *The Gospel of Luke* (Grand Rapids, MI, 1997), p. 450; and John Phillips, *Exploring the Gospel of Luke: An Expository Commentary* (Grand Rapids, MI, 2005), p. 166.

25 R. K. Harrison, 'Heal', in *International Standard Bible Encyclopedia E–J*, ed. Geoffrey W. Bromiley [1915] (Grand Rapids, MI, 1982), p. 644.

26 Benjamin Sass and Joachim Mazahn, *Aramaic and Figural Stamp Impressions on Bricks of the 6th Century BC from Babylon* (Wiesbaden, 2010), p. 182.

27 Tallay Ornan, 'The Queen in Public: Royal Women in Neo-Assyrian Art', in *Sex and Gender in the Ancient Near East*, ed. S. Parpola and R. M. Whiting (Helsinki, 2002), pp. 470–71.

28 Nys, 'Scorpion People', pp. 10–11.

29 Karen Radner, 'The Seal of Tašmetum-šarrat, Sennacherib's Queen, and its Impressions', in *Leggo! Studies Presented to Frederick Mario Fales on the Occasion of His 65th Birthday*, ed. Giovanni B. Lanfranchi et al. (Wiesbaden, 2012), pp. 691–2.

3 THE SCORPION KING

1 Lucia Gahlin, *Egypt: Gods, Myth and Religion* (New York, 2002), p. 312.

2 Melinda K. Hartwig, *Tomb Painting and Identity in Ancient Thebes, 1419–1372 BCE* (Brussels, 2004), pp. 59–60.

3 Rosalie David and Antony E. David, *A Biographical Dictionary of Ancient Egypt* (London, 1992), pp. 127–8.

4 Professor John Baines, personal communication, 6 October 2014.

5 David and David, *A Biographical Dictionary*, p. 128.

6 Professor John Baines, personal communication, 6 October 2014.

7 David O'Connor and David P. Silverman, *Ancient Egyptian Kingship* (Leiden, 1995), p. xxiii.

8 Ibid., p. xxv.

9 Bernard Ziskind and Bruno Halioua, 'Occupational Medicine in Ancient Egypt', *Medical Hypotheses*, LXIX (2007), p. 943.

10 Hisham K. El-Hennawy, 'Scorpions in Ancient Egypt', *Euscorpius*, CXIX (2011), p. 3.

11 Frédérique von Känel, *Les Prêtres-ouâb de Sekhmet et les conjurateurs de Serket* (Paris, 1984).

12 Henri Frankfort, *Kingship and the Gods* (Chicago, IL, 1978), p. 43.

13 Geraldine Pinch, *Handbook of Egyptian Mythology* (Portland, OR, 2003), p. 190; J. F. Borghouts, ed., *Ancient Egyptian Magical Texts* (Leiden, 1978), pp. 69–70, 72.

14 George Hart, *A Dictionary of Egyptian Gods and Goddesses* (London, 1998), p. 212.

15 Charles Russell Coulter and Patricia Turner, *Encyclopaedia of Ancient Deities* (London, 2000), p. 244.

16 Pete Sigal, *The Flower and the Scorpion* (Durham, 2011), pp. 7–9.

17 El-Hennawy, 'Scorpions', p. 3.

18 Pinch, *Handbook of Egyptian Mythology*, p. 145.

19 Sarah Iles Johnston, *Ancient Greek Divination* (Oxford, 2008), pp. 152–3.

20 Suetonius, *The Twelve Caesars*, trans. Robert Graves (London, 2007), p. 63.

21 Janet H. Johnson, trans., 'PDM xiv. 595–607', in *The Greek Magical Papyri in Translation: Including the Demotic Spells*, vol. I: *The Texts*, ed. Hans Dieter Betz (London, 1992), p. 228.

22 See http://museumvictoria.com.au/discoverycentre.

23 Mario Liverani, *Akkad, the First World Empire: Structure, Ideology, Traditions* (Padua, 1993).

24 Zoltán Niederreiter, 'Le Rôle des symboles figurés attribués aux membres de la cour de Sargon II: des emblèmes créés par les lettrés du palais au service de l'idéologie royale', *Iraq*, LXX (2008), p. 51.

25 Mr Zac Phillips, personal communication, 20 October 2014; see Toby Wilkinson, *The Rise and Fall of Ancient Egypt* (London, 2010), p. 43.

26 Wilkinson, *Rise and Fall*, p. 43.

4 THE SCORPION WEAPON

1 Gary R. Mullen and Scott A. Stockwell, 'Scorpions (Scorpiones)', in *Medical and Veterinary Entomology*, ed. Gary R. Mullen and Lance A. Durden (San Diego, CA, 2002), p. 411.

2 Adrienne Mayor, *Greek Fire, Poison Arrows and Scorpion Bombs* (Woodstock, NY, 2003), p. 182.

3 Ibid., p. 185.

4 Jeffrey Alan Lockwood, *Six-legged Soldiers: Using Insects as Weapons of War* (Oxford, 2009), p. 206.

5 Perceval Landon, *Lhasa: The Mysterious City* (Delhi, 1988), p. 147.

6 See L. Mazzotti and M. A. Bravo-Becherella, 'Scorpionism
   in the Mexican Republic', in *Venomous and Poisonous Animals
   and Noxious Plants of the Pacific Region*, ed. H. L. Keegan and
   W. V. Macfarlane (New York, 1963), p. 124; James F. Smith,
   'Durango's Cult of the Scorpion', *Los Angeles Times*
   (22 December 2000).
7 'Scorpions on the Loose in Shenzhen', *Shanghai Daily*,
   www.china.org.cn, 21 July 2011.
8 'Scorpions on the Loose in Shenzhen', *Shanghai Daily*.
9 'Of Thee I Sting', *Phoenix New Times*, www.phoenixnewtimes.com,
   11 August 1993.
10 Mayor, *Greek Fire*, p. 182.
11 Boris Rankov, *The Praetorian Guard* (Oxford, 2001), p. 27.
12 Ibid., pp. 52–3.
13 Robert Beer, *The Handbook of Tibetan Buddhist Symbols* (Chicago,
   IL, 2003), p. 126.
14 Donald J. LaRocca, *Warriors of the Himalayas: Rediscovering the
   Arms and Armor of Tibet* (New York, 2006), p. 40.
15 Beer, *Tibetan Buddhist Symbols*, p. 125.
16 LaRocca, *Warriors of the Himalayas*, p. 40.
17 Beer, *Tibetan Buddhist Symbols*, p. 127.
18 Charles Thorpe, *Oppenheimer: The Tragic Intellect* (Chicago, IL,
   2006), p. 12.
19 J. Robert Oppenheimer, 'Atomic Weapons and American Policy',
   www.foreignaffairs.com, July 1953.
20 Professor James Oakes, personal communication, 3 October 2014.
21 James Oakes, *The Scorpion's Sting: Antislavery and the Coming of the
   Civil War* (New York, 2014), p. 25.
22 Ibid., pp. 25–6.
23 Ibid., p. 26.
24 Professor James Oakes, personal communication, 3 October
   2014.
25 Ibid.
26 Ibid.
27 Lockwood, *Six-legged Soldiers*, p. 291.

28 Luther E. Lindler, Frank J. Lebeda and George Korch, eds, *Biological Weapons Defence: Infectious Disease and Counterbioterrorism* (Totowa, NJ, 2005), p. 274.

29 Mr Zac Phillips, personal communication, 20 October 2014.

5 SCORPIONS IN THE STARS

1 R. Campbell Thompson, 'The Reports of the Magicians and Astrologers of Nineveh and Babylon, *c.* 2500–670 BCE. Part VI: Omens from Halos', www.fordham.edu, accessed April 2014.

2 J. L. Cloudsley-Thompson, 'Scorpions in Mythology, Folklore and History', in *The Biology of Scorpions*, ed. Gary A. Polis (Stanford, CA, 1990), p. 468.

3 W. Deonna, 'Mercure et le scorpion', *Latomus*, XVIII (1959), p. 52.

4 Apollodrous, 'Library', in *Apollodorus' Library and Hyginus' Fabulae: Two Handbooks of Greek Mythology*, trans. R. Scott Smith and Stephen M. Trzaskoma (Cambridge, 2007), p. 69.

5 Liberalis, *The Metamorphoses of Antoninus Liberalis: A Translation with a Commentary*, trans. Francis Celoria (London, 1992), p. 101.

6 For its link to Persian religious imagery, see the 'Marble Group of Mithras Slaying the Bull', www.britishmuseum.org, accessed September 2014; Manfred Clauss, *The Roman Cult of Mithras: The God and his Mysteries*, trans. Richard Gordon (New York, 2001), p. 99.

7 Maryke Steffens, 'Australia's First Astronomers', *ABC Science*, www.abc.net.au, 27 July 2009.

8 Gene Kritsky and Ron Cherry, *Insect Mythology* (San José, CA, 2000), p. 92.

9 Ibid.

10 Mr Ryan Seaman, personal communication, 23 July 2014.

11 Ibid.

12 Ibid.

13 Ibid.

14 Michael Stone, *The Inner Tradition of Yoga* (Boston, MA, 2008), pp. 117–18.

15 Ibid., p. 117.

16 Alanna Kaivalya and Arjuna van der Kooij, *Myths of the Asanas: The Ancient Origins of Yoga* (San Rafael, CA, 2010), p. 16.

17 Ibid.

18 Ms Ashley Turner, personal communication, 8 October 2014.

19 B.K.S. Iyengar, *Light on Yoga* (New York, 1966), p. 388.

20 Ms Ashley Turner, personal communication, 27 September 2014.

21 Ms Ashley Turner, personal communication, 8 October 2014.

22 Ibid.

6 SCORPIONS ON SCREEN AND BEYOND

1 Ian Fleming, *You Only Live Twice* (London, 1964), p. 171.

2 Jacob M. Held and James B. South, eds, *James Bond and Philosophy: Questions are Forever* (Peru, IL, 2006), pp. 66–8.

3 'The Eroticization of Torture in *Die Another Day*', www.criticalcommons.org, accessed July 2014.

4 Nadine Nys, 'Scorpion People: Dangerous or Protective?', *Studia Mesopotamica*, I (2014), pp. 11–13.

5 Jürgen Wasim Frembgen, 'The Scorpion in Muslim Folklore', *Asian Folklore Studies*, LXIII (2004), p. 106.

6 John C. Burnam, *A Soldier's Best Friend: Scout Dogs and their Handlers in the Vietnam War* (New York, 2000), p. 208.

7 Philip C. DiMare, *Movies in American History: An Encyclopedia* (Santa Barbara, CA, 2011), p. 256.

8 Peter Cameron et al., *Textbook of Emergency Paediatric Medicine* (Melbourne, 2012), p. 530.

9 John Freeman, *Life of the Rev. William Kirby* (London, 1852), p. 423.

10 Brantley Bardin, '20Q: Armie Hammer', *Playboy*, www.playboy. com, 21 June 2013.

11 Elliot Logan, 'Interview with *Drive* Director Nicolas Winding Refn', The 500 Club, http://500.the400club.org, 27 October 2011.

12 James H. Bunn, *Wave Forms: A Natural Syntax for Rhythmic Languages* (Stanford, CA, 2002), p. 235.

13 George Wells Ferguson, *Signs and Symbols in Christian Art* (New York, 1961), p. 24.

14 The Art Gallery of Western Australia, 'Conversations on Christ in the Wilderness', www.artgallery.wa.gov.au.

15 John Milton, *Paradise Lost* (1667), at www.dartmouth.edu, accessed 11 December 2015.

16 Frembgen, 'The Scorpion in Muslim Folklore', pp. 103–5.

17 David Waines, *Food Culture and Health in Pre-modern Muslim Societies* (Leiden, 2011), p. 247.

18 Allison Lee Palmer, *Historical Dictionary of Neoclassical Art and Architecture* (Plymouth, MA, 2011), p. 30.

19 Ibid.

20 State Hermitage Museum, 'Hermitage History: A Walk Through the Imperial Hermitage', www.hermitagemuseum.org, accessed June 2014.

21 Bristol Street Art Gallery, www.bristol-street-art.co.uk, accessed July 2014.

22 Virginia Woolf, *The Common Reader* [1925] (New York, 1984), p. 182.

23 George Gordon Byron, *The Giaour: A Fragment of a Turkish Tale* (London, 1813), p. 8.

24 Ourania Chatsiou, 'Lord Byron: Paratext and Poetics', *Modern Language Review*, CIX (2014), p. 10.

25 Nissim Ezekiel, 'Night of the Scorpion', in *Modern Indian Literature: An Anthology*, ed. K. M. George (New Delhi, 1992), pp. 546–7.

26 Kenneth Muir, *Shakespeare's Tragic Sequence* (London, 1972), p. 121.

27 Mark Dominik, *William Shakespeare and the Birth of Merlin* (Beaverton, OR, 1991), p. 154.

28 Sir Arthur Conan Doyle, *The Complete Sherlock Holmes* (London, 2012), pp 389 and 2179.

29 Frank Mastropolo, 'An Internment Camp within an Internment Camp', *ABC News*, http://abcnews.go.com, 19 February 2008.

30 See http://annika.new.mu.nu, accessed 20 November 2015.

1 Kathlyn Gay and Christine Whittington, *Body Marks: Tattooing, Piercing and Scarification* (Hong Kong, 2002), p. 21.

2 Clinton Sanders, *Customising the Body* (Philadelphia, PA, 1989), p. 208.

3 G. A. Pearson, 'Insect Tattoos on Humans: A "Dermagraphic" Study', *American Entomologist*, XXXI (1996), p. 100.

4 Ibid.

5 Ibid., p. 103.

6 Jennifer S. Holland, 'The Bite That Heals', http://ngm. nationalgeographic.com, accessed September 2014.

7 Kartik Sunagar et al., 'Evolution Stings: The Origin and Diversification of Scorpion Toxin Peptide Scaffolds', *Toxins*, V (2013), pp. 2456–87.

8 C. A. Hernández-Aponte et al., 'Vejovine, A New Antibiotic from the Scorpion Venom of *Vaejovis mexicanus*', *Toxicon*, LVII (2011), pp. 84–92.

9 Emily Sohn, 'Scorpion Venom Tapped as Pesticide', www.abc.net. au, 20 January 2010.

10 Hannah Waters, 'Fungus Fights Malaria?', *The Scientist*, 24 February 2011.

11 J. Ding et al., 'Scorpion Venoms as a Potential Source of Novel Cancer Therapeutic Compounds', *Experimental Biology and Medicine*, CCXXXIX (2014), pp. 387–93.

12 Douglas Main, 'Fighting Cancer with Scorpion and Honeybee Venom', www.newsweek.com, 8 August 2014.

13 E. H. Kern, 'My Favourite Animal, The Book Scorpion', www.bookriot.com, 6 June 2015.

14 Julian Bohne, 'Can Mini Scorpions Save the Dying Bee?', www.dw.de, 8 June 2015.

15 Ibid.

16 See www.speciesconservation.org, accessed September 2014.

17 Mr Robert Blackburn, personal communication, 23 September 2014.

18 See http://scorpion.amnh.org, accessed October 2014.

19 Professor Lorenzo Prendini, personal communication,
    19 September 2014.

20 Mr Robert Blackburn, personal communication,
    23 September 2014.

21 See http://scorpion.amnh.org, accessed October 2014.

22 Yury Fedotov and John E. Scanlon, 'Wildlife Crime Ranks Among
    Trafficking in Drugs, Arms and Humans', www.theguardian.com,
    27 September 2013.

23 Ibid.

24 Mr Paul Maguire, personal communication, 16 October 2014.

25 Mr Paul Maguire, personal communication, 17 October 2014.

26 Mr Paul Maguire, personal communication, 16 October 2014.

27 Ragnhild Sollund, 'The Victimisation of Women, Children and
    Non-human Species through Trafficking and Trade: Crimes
    Understood through an Ecofeminist Perspective', in *Routledge
    International Handbook of Green Criminology*, ed. Nigel South and
    Avi Brisman (New York, 2013), p. 322.

28 Tanya Wyatt, 'Uncovering the Significance of and Motivation for
    Wildlife Trafficking', in *Routledge International Handbook of Green
    Criminology*, ed. South and Brisman, p. 302.

29 James Griffiths, 'Chinese Authorities Find Almost 100 "Man-killer"
    Scorpions in Parcels sent from Germany', www.scmp.com, 16
    September 2014.

30 Professor Lorenzo Prendini, personal communication,
    19 September 2014.

31 W. David Sissom and Brent E. Hendrixson, 'Scorpion Biodiversity
    and Patterns of Endemism in Northern Mexico', in *Biodiversity,
    Ecosystems and Conservation in Northern Mexico*, ed. Jean-Luc E.
    Cartron, Gerardo Ceballos and Richard Stephen Felger (New York,
    2005), p. 135.

32 Ibid.

33 Sollund, 'Victimisation', p. 322.

34 Faiza Ilyas, 'Wildlife Dept Moves after Months of Illegal Scorpion
    Hunting Across Country', www.dawn.com, 22 July 2014.

35 Daniel A. Medina, 'A Look at Pakistan's Amazingly Lucrative
    Scorpion Trade', www.qz.com, 8 October 2014.

36 Maham Javaid, 'The Scorpion Hunters of Pakistan', www.aljazeera.
    com, 8 October 2014.

37 Ilyas, 'Scorpion Hunting'.

38 Professor Lorenzo Prendini, personal communication,
    19 September 2014.

39 'Scorpion Venom: Bad for Bugs, Good for Pesticides',
    www.sciencedaily.com, 27 April 2011.

40 'The Old Man and the Scorpion' available at Stony Brook
    University Club website, www.ic.sunysb.edu, accessed
    13 September 2014.

Bibliography

Anderson, R. C., *Scorpions, The Ancient Arachnids* (Pocatello, ID, 1983)

Dupré, G., *Des Scorpions et des hommes: Une Histoire de la scorpionologie de l'antiquité à nos jours* (Villeneuve St Georges, 2008)

—, *Worldwide Bibliography of Scorpions, Second Edition* (2013), available from www.ntnu.no/ub/scorpion-files/dupre_2013.pdf

Fet, V., and P. A. Selden, *Scorpions 2001: In Memoriam Gary A. Polis* (Burnham Beeches, Bucks, 2001)

Gopalakrishnakone, P., et al., eds, *Scorpion Venoms* (Houten, 2015)

Keegan, H. L., *Scorpions of Medical Importance* (Jackson, MS, 1980)

Kritsky, G., and R. Cherry, *Insect Mythology* (San Jose, CA, 2000)

Mahsberg, D., R. Lippe and S. Kallas, *Skorpione: Lebensraum, Haltung, Zucht* (Münster, 2012)

Polis, G. A., ed., *The Biology of Scorpions* (Stanford, CA, 1990)

Pringle, L., *Scorpion Man: Exploring the World of Scorpions* (New York, 1994)

Stockmann, R., and E. Ythier, *Scorpions of the World* (Verrières-le-Buisson, 2010)

Associations and Websites

American Arachnological Society
www.americanarachnology.org

Arachnodata, The Arachnological Research and Consulting Agency
www.arachnodata.ch

Australasian Arachnological Society
www.australasian-arachnology.org

British Arachnological Society
www.britishspiders.org.uk

Euscorpius Journal, Occasional Publications in Scorpiology
http://science.marshall.edu/fet/euscorpius

International Society of Arachnology
http://arachnology.org

Journal of Arachnology online
www.americanarachnology.org/JOA_online.html

Scorpion Systematics Research Group in the Division of Invertebrate Zoology at the American Museum of Natural History (AMNH)
http://scorpion.amnh.org/index.html

Scorpions World
www.scorpionsworld.fr

The Scorpion Files
www.ntnu.no/ub/scorpion-files

Acknowledgements

I would like to thank my former student and beloved friend, Damien Stone, for his encouragement to write on scorpions. I would also like to thank my dear friends and colleagues for their help and support, especially Zac Phillips, Ian Young, Dane Drivas, Tom Kennedy, Ande Cunningham, Emma Barlow, Brennan Nicholson, Marija Elektra Rodriguez and Sam Grosser. Thanks to my delightful students at the University of Sydney, for their unfailing patience with my frequent scorpion-infused digressions in the classroom.

Many distinguished experts and scholars generously gave their time and advice in the composition of this book: my deep gratitude to Lorenzo Prendini, Robert Blackburn, Rob Gess, James Oakes, Nadine Nys, John Baines, Ashley Turner, Ryan Seaman and Paul Maguire. My thanks to the series editor, Jonathan Burt, and to Michael Leaman for their advice and help. Thanks to Susannah Jayes and Amy Salter, who both provided generous assistance in improving this volume. I greatly appreciate the invaluable help of Ann Sylph and James Godwin at the Zoological Society of London, who found so many beautiful pictures. I would like to express my gratitude for the generosity of the Nicholson Museum at the University of Sydney, especially Elizabeth Bollen, and for the help of Taronga Zoo.

Photo Acknowledgements

The author and the publishers wish to express their thanks to the below sources of illustrative material and /or permission to reproduce it.

Airwolfhound: p. 119; Anabis_n: p. 24; An-d: p. 187; Andytang20: p. 177; © Ashmolean Museum, University of Oxford: pp. 81, 82; BafS – this file is licensed under the Creative Commons Attribution-Share Alike 3.0 Unported License – readers are free to share – to copy, distribute and transmit the work – to remix – to adapt the work – under the following conditions – attribution – you must attribute the work in the manner specified by the author or licensor, but not in any way that suggests that they endorse you or your use of the work – share alike – if you alter, transform, or build upon this work, you may distribute the resulting work only under the same or similar license to this one: p. 34; Michael Baird: p. 186; Berlin State Museums: p. 76 right; © The Trustees of the British Museum, London: p. 156; Tomas Castelazo: p. 30; Jayendra Chiplunkar: p. 16 bottom; Cornell Collection of Antiquities: p. 164; Didier Descouens: p. 14; FelixReimann: p. 39; Ginny Freeman: p. 189; courtesy Robert W. Gess, 2013: pp. 57, 58; The J. Paul Getty Museum, Los Angeles: p. 71 (Ms. Ludwig xv 4, fol. 119v), 148 (Ms. 20, fol. 53); Davidgoehring: p. 142; Ghedoghedo: p. 56; Hectonichus: p. 52; HTO: p. 10; Chris Huh: p. 12; InSapphoWeTrust: p. 171; iStock: pp. 6 (JanPietruska), 40 (Woodkern), 42 (TaneryILDIRIM), 120 (risamay), 144 (missyas), 180 (cosmin), 188 (Crissy1982); Kmo5ap: p. 25; Dakota L.: p. 36; Library of Congress, Washington, DC: p. 134; Conny Liegel: p. 162; Los Angeles Museum of Art: p. 115 (from the Nasli and Alice

Heeramaneck Collection, Museum Associates Purchase [M.83.105.17]; courtesy Los Angeles County Museum of Art (LACMA): p. 144 bottom; Mark Marathon – Travail personnel: p. 143; Nicholson Museum, University of Sydney: pp. 91 (NMR.344.1-2), 114 top left (NM2004.276); Carole Raddato: p. 131; REX Shutterstock: pp. 98 (Moviestore), 99 (Universal/Everett), 149 (Everett), 153 (Everett); courtesy Ryan Seaman: p. 139; Dominic Sherony: p. 37; Shutterstock: pp. 11 (skydie), 21 (Patricia Chumillas), 35 (Sainam51), 45 (Arnoud Quanjer), 49 (Peter Bay), 87 (mountainpix), 122 (Digital Storm), 166 (Audrey Snider Bell), 170 (Mikhail Egorov), 174 (IrinaK), 175 (KPG_Euro); Siga: p. 18 top; State Hermitage Museum, St Petersburg: p. 160; Hans Stieglit: p. 133; Olaf Tausch: p. 80; U.S. National Park Service: p. 33 (Robb Hannawacker); Victoria and Albert Museum, London: p. 76 left; Michel Wal: p. 68; Kevin Walsh: p. 185; courtesy Walters Art Museum, Baltimore: pp. 63, 88, 93, 125, 167; Philipp Weigell: pp. 13, 18 bottom; Wellcome Library, London: pp. 108, 112; H. Zell: p. 59; Zoological Society of London: pp. 9, 16 top, 19, 22, 23, 26, 29, 55, 104, 105, 135, 190.

Index